Creature Feature Devotions for Children's Ministry

Loveland, Colorado

Creature Feature Devotions for Children's Ministry
Copyright © 2001 Group Publishing, Inc.

Visit our Web site: **www.grouppublishing.com**

Credits

Contributing Authors: Jacqui Baker, Sarah Macy Bohrer, Chip Borgstadt, Katy Borgstadt, Karen Choi, Neil Dyer, Katie Garcia, Sheila Halasz, Julie Lavender, Pamela Malloy, and Paul Woods
Book Acquisitions Editor: Linda A. Anderson
Editor: Alison Imbriaco
Chief Creative Officer: Joani Schultz
Copy Editor: Deirdre Brouer
Art Director: Jean Bruns
Designer: Ministrybeehive Christian Design Services
Cover Art Director: Jeff A. Storm
Cover Designer: Coonts Design Group, LLC
Cover Illustrator: David Merrell
Illustrators: Pamela Johnson and David Gagné
Production Manager: Peggy Naylor

Library of Congress Cataloging-in-Publication Data
Creature feature devotions for children's ministry.
    p. cm.
  Includes index.
  ISBN 0-7644-2229-4 (alk. paper)
  1. Virtues--Study and teaching (Elementary) 2. Christian education of children.
BV4630 .C74 2001
268'.432--dc21   00-042965

10 9 8 7 6 5 4 3 2 1   10 09 08 07 06 05 04 03 02 01

Printed in the United States of America.

TABLE OF CONTENTS

INTRODUCTION

What, exactly, *is* perseverance…loyalty…or compassion? And how can you teach these abstract concepts to elementary-age children?

Creature Feature Devotions for Children's Ministry gives you a variety of quick answers. These devotions will help children experience such abstract character traits as initiative, courage, and responsibility in ways they can understand.

The devotions capture children's attention by building on their natural fascination with animal behavior. Specific facts about animal behavior bring abstract concepts down to earth. And easy-to-do, active-learning exercises help children discover and explore the concepts in real-life terms.

In each devotion, you'll find open-ended questions to bring children into a meaningful and personal discussion that will help them understand how the character trait relates to their own behavior and the behavior they see around them. A Bible passage then helps the children understand the concept in spiritual terms. Finally, the devotion challenges children to apply what they've learned as they do something specific and immediate.

To lead your children into deeper walks with God, use these devotions for children's sermons, Sunday school, after-school programs, vacation Bible school, and any other settings in which children are gathered.

COMPASSION

 Starring the HEN

Plot Point: Jesus wants us to care for and reach out to people who don't know God.

Props: You'll need a Bible, an umbrella, and a large blanket.

Setting the Stage: Have the children sit in a semicircle.

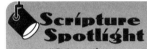
 Action!

ASK:

• **Are you ready to do a little acting?**

Ask for volunteers to act the parts of a cold wind and a thunderstorm. (Several children can play each part.) You'll also need one child to be an umbrella holder and another to be a blanket holder. Divide the rest of the group into two teams of weather victims/observers. (When the teams are not weather victims, they'll be observers.)

Have the first team of weather victims and the cold wind come to the front. Encourage the kids to act their parts with lots of huffing and puffing, if they are the wind, and, if they are weather victims, lots of shivering and teeth chattering.

ASK:

• **What do you think, observers? How do you think our weather victims feel?**

• **What should we do? Should we let them stand out there and freeze?**

• **How can we help them?**

When observers have suggested remedies, such as wrapping the weather victims in a blanket or inviting them in out of the cold, thank the actors, and have them sit.

Then have the second weather victim team and the thunderstorm actors come to the front. Encourage lots of booming, crackling, and whooshing from the thunderstorm. If several children are playing the part, suggest that one be lightning, another be thunder, and another be rain. Encourage the weather victims to act soggy and soaked.

ASK:

- **What should we do, observers? Do we want them to get wet?**
- **How do you think they feel?**
- **How can we help?**

When observers have suggested giving the weather victims an umbrella, thank the actors, and have them sit.

ASK:

- **Do you know what word describes helping someone out of a bad situation into a good situation, especially when you know what it feels like in that bad situation?**

SAY: Wanting to help someone who needs help is called *compassion*. When you want others to have what is good for them, you're feeling *compassion*.

Jesus knows how good it is for people to live with God. When he sees people without God, he feels *compassion* for them. Jesus wants all people to have God in their lives because he wants what is good for them. Listen to what Jesus said about the city of Jerusalem. At that time, many people living in Jerusalem did not know God.

Read aloud Luke 13:34, then show children the illustration (p. 9) of the chicks running for cover under the hen's wings.

ASK:

- **Why do you suppose the hen has her wings over the chicks?**
- **Why does she look after them so carefully?**

SAY: The hen gives the chicks a warm, dry, safe place because she cares about her family. Jesus feels the same way about his family. He wants to take care of people by bringing them to him.

 **Zoom In**

ASK:

- **What would have happened to the weather victims if you had not given them the blanket and umbrella?**
- **When has someone shown *compassion* toward you? How did it make you feel?**
- **What have you done to show *compassion* to someone? How did that make you feel?**

 Finale

Have about half of the children join hands and form a circle around the rest of the children to suggest the atmosphere of a safe huddle. Stand outside the huddle.

SAY: To those of us who know God, being in his family is sort of like being safely gathered in this close huddle. Jesus wants to be everyone's safe place in the same way that a mother hen wants to gather her chicks under her wings.

Think of someone you should feel *compassion* for. Do you have a friend or brother or sister who needs you to understand and care? How could you show *compassion* to that person this week? What can you do to help the person feel that God cares about him or her?

Let's talk to God about it.

PRAY: Dear God, we are so thankful to be a part of your family. Thank you for showing *compassion* toward us. And now, God, we're asking you to help us show *compassion* to others. When we see people who need our care, people who need your love, please give us the courage to help them. We ask this in Jesus' name, amen.

Starring the REINDEER

Plot Point: God gives us strength to protect our weaker brothers and sisters.

Props: You'll need a Bible, paper, pencils, and a picture of reindeer or caribou.

Setting the Stage: Have the kids form two teams, and designate a Team A and a Team B. Have each team choose one person to protect.

Scripture Spotlight

"Love always protects, always trusts, always hopes, always perseveres" (1 Corinthians 13:7).

 Action!

SAY: We're going to play a game called the Reindeer Game, which is a little like the game Red Rover. Each team has selected one person to protect. The rest of the team should form a line and link arms.

Team A, you'll say, "Reindeer, reindeer send so-and-so over," naming someone from Team B. That person will unlink arms and rush over to Team A's line. The goal is to break through the line and tag the protected person behind the line.

If the person you called does break through, he or she will return to Team B with the protected person, and Team A must select a new person to protect. If the person you call fails to break through the line, that person will join your team. Then it will be Team B's turn to call someone over.

Allow time for kids to play the game. Then have them sit in a semi-circle, and show them the picture of reindeer.

Director's Notes

If you can, show the kids a set of deer antlers. (Contact your state or county fish-and-game or wildlife department, and ask if that office has a display that can be borrowed.) Be sure to point out the differences between deer antlers and those of reindeer. Reindeer antlers are larger and shaped differently.

SAY: Reindeer have a way of protecting weaker reindeer that's similar to the way you protected your team member. When reindeer sense a predator, they'll try to outrun it. If some of the reindeer are too old, too sick, or too young to outrun the danger, though, stronger reindeer will often protect them. For example, when wolves attack the reindeer herd, the stronger reindeer form a circle around the weaker reindeer. Both male and female reindeer have very large antlers. When the stronger reindeer walk around the outside of the circle, they make a wall of antlers to protect the old, sick, or very young reindeer. Usually, the wolves will give up and go away.

God wants us to care for and protect each other just as the reindeer do. Wanting to care for and protect someone is called *compassion*. When someone is weak, God wants us to help that person be safe and secure. And he wants us to help each other be secure and strong in our faith.

Read 1 Corinthians 13:7 to the children.

Zoom In

ASK:

- Who do you feel *compassion* for?
- Why might they need to be protected?
- What are some ways we can help the people we love feel secure?
- How can we help people feel strong in their faith?

Finale

Pass out paper and pencils.

SAY: Make a list or draw a picture of ways you could stand up for or protect your friends and family. If you make a list, put a star next to the items you can do during the coming week.

Starring the ELEPHANT

Plot Point: We need to help those weaker than we are.

Props: You'll need a Bible, masking tape, index cards, and pencils.

Setting the Stage: Use masking tape to mark a start and a finish line on the floor.

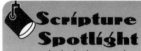

Scripture Spotlight

"I needed clothes and you clothed me, I was sick and you looked after me, I was in prison and you came to visit me" (Matthew 25:36).

 Action!

Form teams of three, and explain to the children that they are going to play a game called Get the Elephant to the Water Hole. Depending on the size of your group and the size of your room, you may want to have all the teams stand along the start line to begin at the same time, or you may choose to have one team go at a time.

SAY: Here are the rules of this game: One person on each team will be the weak elephant, and the other two people will be strong elephants. The strong elephants will stand on either side of the weak elephant, standing close enough to touch arms with the weak elephant. When I give the signal, you must get to the water hole at the finish line. The weak elephant can't get there alone, though, so the strong elephants will have to support the weak elephant by keeping their arms in contact with the weak elephant's arms. If you lose contact along the way, you'll have to go back and start again. The goal is to get all the elephants to the water hole.

When everyone has made it to the finish line,

SAY: We know that elephants take care of each other. For example, if one elephant is too weak or tired to make it to water, two stronger elephants will help the weaker elephant, just as we practiced doing. The strong elephants will stand on either side of the weaker elephant and push their bodies against the weaker elephant to support it and help it to water. Helping someone else to the water hole is a lot more difficult than just going by yourself, isn't it?

Read Matthew 25:36 to the children.

 Zoom In

SAY: When we want to take care of someone who's weaker than we are, we're feeling compassion for that person.
ASK:

- **Think of times you have felt like the weak elephant. What kinds of help would you have liked?**

- Think of times you have felt strong. How could you use your strength to help someone else?
- How can we take care of each other the way the elephants do?

Finale

Distribute index cards and pencils.

SAY: Think of someone who is weak and could use your help. Then think about how you could help that person during the coming week. On your index card, make a note or draw a picture of how you could help that person. Keep the card with you during the week as a reminder.

Starring the CANADA GOOSE

Plot Point: God wants us to care about each other.

Props: You'll need a Bible.

Setting the Stage: Clear space in the room for a game of Tag.

Scripture Spotlight
"The entire law is summed up in a single command: 'Love your neighbor as yourself'" (Galatians 5:14).

 Action!

Choose one person to be the hunter and another to be the goose. Have the other children form pairs and hold hands.

SAY: This goose will be looking for a safe place because the hunter is after it. For this goose, holding hands with any of you means safety. But as soon as the goose takes someone's hand, that person's partner will have to drop hands and be the goose!

If you're holding someone's hand, stand still, but reach out as far as you can to the goose. If the hunter tags the goose, the goose becomes the hunter and chooses a new goose.

After several minutes, have the children sit in a semicircle.

SAY: Canada geese will do anything they can to help their partners and their families. They will give their lives to "reach out" to each other. People have noticed that if a goose is shot down by a hunter as the flock is migrating south, its mate will circle back, risking death, to help its partner. If one partner is wounded, the other will remain with it until it's healed. If one goose can't be found when the flock begins its journey south, that goose's partner will stay behind to wait for it, even if that means being alone in the freezing weather while it looks for its partner.

The geese do all they can to take care of their partners and their goslings. But the Bible tells us we are part of a larger family.

Read Galatians 5:14 to the children.

ASK:

• Who are our neighbors?

SAY: God wants us to help others when they are weak or in trouble just as we would want someone to help us.

 Zoom In

ASK:

• How are the ways geese show *compassion* like the ways we can show *compassion*? How are they different?
• What are some ways we can reach out to each other?
• Who are some people we should reach out to?

Finale

SAY: Find a partner, then share with your partner one thing you will do this week to help someone.

COURAGE

 Starring the **DACHSHUND**

Plot Point: Sometimes it takes *courage* to trust God and wait.

Props: You'll need a Bible, a picture of a dachshund, napkins, and tasty treats that the kids will not want to wait to eat.

Setting the Stage: Have the treats ready to show and serve, and have the picture close by.

Scripture Spotlight
"Wait for the Lord; be strong and take heart and wait for the Lord" (Psalm 27:14).

 Action!

Show kids the treats you've brought. If they smell good, let kids smell them. But don't let kids take them or eat them yet.

SAY: In a little while, you're going to get to eat these treats—but not just yet. They look very good, don't they?

Set the treats in front of the class, and read the following information about dachshunds.

SAY: Dachshunds were originally bred to hunt badgers. They are feisty little dogs that aren't afraid of facing an animal that could tear apart a much bigger dog.

Show the picture of the dachshund, and ask children approximately how big a dachshund is and how much it weighs. (A full-size dachshund usually stands about nine inches high at the shoulder and weighs between sixteen and thirty-two pounds. Miniature dachshunds weigh eleven pounds or less.)

SAY: Dachshunds don't fight mean animals by attacking the animal head-on. A dachshund can get the better of a raccoon more than twice its weight by waiting. Someone once saw a dachshund fighting a raccoon. The dachshund would wait, then backpedal when the raccoon advanced, circle around behind the raccoon, and nip it from behind. Circling, waiting, and nipping at just the right time—again and again—the dachshund caused the raccoon to become so worn out and bewildered that it didn't know what to do.

Sometimes we think we have to attack things head-on to show *courage*. But sometimes that means running ahead of God into almost certain defeat. God wants us to rely fully on him, and sometimes that means waiting and being wise about when to make a move—just like the dachshund facing the raccoon. In a few more minutes, we'll have the treats, but first, can any of you tell us any more about dachshunds?

Wait for kids to respond. Continue to question them about dachshunds for a few minutes. If no one has any comments, you might tell kids that dachshunds come in three varieties: smooth-coat, long-coat, and wire-haired. You might also mention that dachshunds are related to basset hounds.

SAY: I know you'd probably all like to wait longer for the treats, but I think we'll have them now—unless someone objects. Wait a few seconds to see if anyone objects, then distribute the treats and let children eat.

SAY: You probably all realize that I've made you wait for the treats intentionally. Sometimes we need to wait. Sometimes God wants us to wait and trust in him. Read Psalm 27:14 to the children.

 **Zoom In**

ASK:
- **What was it like to wait for the treats?**
- **How is that like waiting for the Lord?**
- **How is waiting for the Lord like the dachshund waiting for the right time to strike?**
- **Why does it sometimes take *courage* to wait?**

 Finale

Have kids form groups of about four to discuss the following questions.
ASK:
- **When has it taken *courage* for you to wait on God for something?**
- **How did that situation turn out?**
- **How can we know that we can trust God when we need to wait?**

SAY: It isn't always easy to wait for God. It takes *courage*, and it takes faith in him. But when we give him time to work, we can always be sure he'll take care of us!

Starring the WOLVERINE

Plot Point: Because of God's power, we can have *courage* in the face of danger.

Props: You'll need a Bible.

Setting the Stage: Set up the room so that there is a place where groups of four can do their freeze-frame poses.

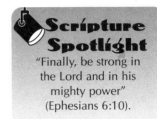

Scripture Spotlight

"Finally, be strong in the Lord and in his mighty power" (Ephesians 6:10).

 Action!

Have children form groups of four. Have members of each group decide together what might be the most dangerous situation they might ever face. The children might think of being confronted by mean guys at night in a dark alley or serving as a soldier in a war. When all groups have chosen a situation, have them prepare to describe it to the rest of the class and to come up with a way to depict the situation by posing in freeze-frame action. When groups are ready, choose a group to describe the situation and then pose. As group members hold their pose,

ASK:

- **What should you do in this situation: move forward or retreat?**

After several kids have answered, move on to the next group and repeat the process, again ending with the question. Keep going until all groups have presented their situations.

SAY: Your situations were very scary! It takes *courage* to move forward in the face of danger. Let's hear about an animal that seems to always have the *courage* to move forward, no matter how dangerous the situation.

The wolverine is a fierce little animal that will fight other animals more than three times its size. Wolverines seem to be very intelligent as well as fearless. They have been known to follow lines of traps people have set and devour the animals caught in the traps. Sometimes they even manage to steal the bait from traps without getting caught.

Though wolverines weigh only about thirty-five pounds, they are persistent little animals. They are not afraid to attack a moose or a deer and are often successful.

Even when faced by a grizzly bear seeking to take away food killed by the wolverine, this little animal will not back down. Instead it will leap at the throat of the bear, trying to kill the bear before the bear's sharp claws and teeth make a quick end of the little wolverine. Never giving up, the wolverine will use its last ounce of strength to continue to attack rather than retreat.

Show children the illustration of the wolverine and the bear below and let them see how much bigger a bear is.

 Zoom In

ASK:

- How is the *courage* of the wolverine like the *courage* needed to face the situations we described earlier? How is it different?

SAY: God tells us that we have a source of *courage* other than ourselves. Let's read Ephesians 6:10.

Read Ephesians 6:10 to the children.

ASK:

- What are some ways God's strength can give you *courage*?
- How is that *courage* similar to the wolverine's? How is it different?

 Finale

Have groups think of what God might want them to do in each of the situations they described earlier. Remind kids that sometimes *courage* involves trusting God and waiting rather than always moving forward. God wants us to have *courage* but doesn't want us to take foolish risks. Discuss each situation one at a time, and get several ideas for each one. Have kids determine if each idea is a good way of trusting in God's power or if it would be a foolish risk.

Close the devotion by asking God to help kids determine how to have *courage* and trust in his power in every situation.

Plot Point: We can look to God for the *courage* to do what we know we should do.

Props: You'll need a Bible, a picture of a robin, and a plastic or metal spoon for each child.

Setting the Stage: Before the class, practice the spoon trick to be sure you can demonstrate it and help the children do it.

 Action!

ASK:

- **What's the hardest thing you've ever done?**

Give children a few minutes to discuss their challenges.

SAY: I have a difficult task for you now. Show children the spoon. **Try to hang the spoon from the end of your nose while you look straight ahead.**

Give each child a spoon, and allow time for children to work at the task.

SAY: Hanging a spoon from the end of your nose seems impossible, doesn't it? We often face problems and situations in our lives that seem impossible. This task is possible, though.

Lick your finger, and rub it on the tip of your nose. Then breathe heavily on the bowl of the spoon. Wait a moment, then hang the tip of the spoon on your nose. Let the spoon balance in place for several seconds, then remove it. Show the children how the trick is done, and let them try it.

ASK:

- **How did you feel about trying something that didn't seem possible?**
- **What are some things you've learned to do that seemed impossible before you learned how to do them?**

SAY: It takes *courage* to try to do something that seems impossible.

ASK:

- **When I say the word *courage*, what is the first animal you think of?**

SAY: I didn't hear anyone mention the robin! Show children the robin picture or, if it's a nice day and you have time, take children outside to look for a robin.

Does the robin look like an animal you would consider to be *courageous*? The robin may not be the first animal you think of when you think of *courage*, but, believe it or not, robins are very *courageous*! When there are baby robins in the nest, the parent will protect them and fight other birds that may try to attack. Robins even have a special call, the teek-call, to warn other birds to keep their distance. It sounds something like this. Repeat a short, shrill *teek teek teek* noise several times. **Let's all make the robin's warning call together.**

Allow children to make the call several times.

Not only do the robins make a warning call, they also dive at any intruder, snapping their bills and making a clicking sound as they dart back and forth. The robin doesn't back down from bigger enemies.
ASK:

- **What are some birds or animals that might try to take eggs or baby birds from the robin's nest?**

Listen for mentions of the raptors (predator birds), as well as crows and cats. Help children understand the difference between a robin, which is usually ten inches in size, and, for example, a crow, which is usually nineteen or twenty inches long.
ASK:

- **How would you feel if you had to drive away something twice as big as you? Do you think it would be impossible?**

SAY: **Robins don't think about whether it's difficult or dangerous to drive away a bigger bird—even one with talons, such as a hawk! Robins do what they can: diving, snapping, clicking, and trying to outmaneuver their opponents. The little robins have the *courage* to believe they can drive away fierce and large intruders.**
ASK:

- **Where can you go to find the *courage* to do what seems impossible?**

Read Deuteronomy 33:27 to the children.
SAY: **In the Bible, God says that when we are scared and lack *courage* we should remember that he is with us wherever we go.**

 Zoom In

ASK:

- **When are you most afraid? What can you do in a situation like that?**
- **How do you feel knowing that God is always with you and will give you *courage* when you are afraid?**
- **How can you rely on God's help with challenges you're facing today?**

 Finale

SAY: **Think of a situation right now in which you need to be *courageous*. Ask God to give you the *courage* you need to bravely face this situation.** Allow children a minute to sit silently and pray.

Starring the MONGOOSE

Plot Point: We should have the *courage* to use the resources we have when faced with overwhelming odds.

Props: You'll need a Bible, a copy of the handout (pp. 25-26), paper, pencils or markers, index cards, a picture of a mongoose, and a rubber snake (a cobra, if possible).

Setting the Stage: Have the rubber snake and the photo nearby to show the children.

 Action!

ASK:
- **How many of you have ever felt scared?**
- **Have you ever felt that you were in an impossible situation with no way out?**
- **Have you ever faced overwhelming odds?**

Allow time for responses, then hold up the rubber snake.
- **How many of you are scared of snakes?**

Hold up the photo of the mongoose.

> ### Scripture Spotlight
> "He gives strength to the weary and increases the power of the weak. Even youths grow tired and weary, and young men stumble and fall; but those who hope in the Lord will renew their strength. They will soar on wings like eagles; they will run and not grow weary, they will walk and not be faint" (Isaiah 40:29-31).

SAY: This is a mongoose. It is a small animal, approximately a foot to one and a half feet long with a long tail. Approximate this size with your hands. **You might think this mongoose isn't much of a match for a snake as big as the cobra. But it kills and eats big snakes. The mongoose doesn't think about being afraid of the snake or whether it's fighting against overwhelming odds. God gave it the resources it needs to be able to kill the snake: speed, quick reflexes, and agility. God has given us resources to use when we face what seems to be overwhelming odds or impossible situations. Today we are going to learn about four people who met some pretty overwhelming odds.**

Have children count off from one to four, and have all the ones go to one corner of the room, all the twos go to another corner, all the threes to another area, and all the fours to a fourth area. Give each team one of the four stories on the handout, paper, and pencils or markers.

SAY: In your group, choose a "reader" and a "scribe." After the reader reads the story aloud, discuss the overwhelming odds or impossible situations the person in the story had to overcome and the resources God gave the person. The scribe can take notes of the group's discussion. After a few minutes, we will get together in one large group to share the information. Allow time for the groups to complete their tasks, then have kids gather in a circle. Ask the scribes from each team to report the team's findings, then ask each group this question:

- **If you were in this person's shoes, what would you have done?**

After groups have shared, read Isaiah 40:29-31 to the children.

Zoom In

ASK:

- **What kind of overwhelming odds do you face?**
- **How are those situations like the overwhelming odds a mongoose faces when fighting a cobra?**
- **What resources does God give you to help you when facing your overwhelming odds?**

Finale

Have the children find partners.

SAY: **Think of a time you need *courage* to deal with a situation that seems impossible. Share your impossible situation with your partner. After your partner has shared a situation with you, quietly ask the Lord to help your partner.**

Seeds of Hope

The sixth graders at San Miguel School in Camden, New Jersey are used to seeing the abandoned buildings and litter-filled vacant lots that are common in the poorer parts of too many cities. But eight sixth-grade students decided to change the way things were.

They began by clearing trash from the vacant lot next to the school. Then they painted signs and planted seeds. The sixth graders hope their efforts will impress the owner of the boarded-up building on the other side of the vacant lot. They want permission to fix up that building next.

The sixth graders explained, "Drugs and pollution make our neighborhood dirty and ugly. If we save our place, it might be a sign of hope for the neighborhood."

One student admitted, "We're eight small kids in a very big world, changing it one step at a time."

Excerpted from *TIME for Kids,* Spring 2000

Save the Fish!

For eight-year-old Aubrey Stahl, the smell was a real problem. Even more of a problem, though, was the 2,000 dead fish floating in the little lake behind her home in Loveland, Colorado. Aubrey wanted to know why all the fish had suddenly died.

Aubrey did some research and learned what makes a lake a healthy home for fish. One thing she learned is that fish need the oxygen produced by plants in the water.

When she was ten, Aubrey started a campaign to educate her neighbors about how to take care of the lake. She distributed brochures that suggested simple things people could do—or not do—to make the lake healthier for the fish. For example, the brochures advised people not to fertilize lawns close to the lake because the chemicals in the fertilizer can harm water plants. The brochures also suggested keeping grass and garbage out of the lake because, as the garbage is rotting in the water, it absorbs oxygen.

Excerpted from *TIME for Kids,* Spring 2000

Encouraging Courage

Receiving a "Most Courageous Athlete" award from a regional association of athletic coaches would be an honor for any high school senior. For Michael Herbst, who graduated from New Jersey's West Deptford High School, the honor was especially hard-earned.

Michael, who has Down's Syndrome, was a disabilities swimmer with the swim and dive team for four years. His athletic ability earned a place at the annual U.S. Swimming Disabilities swim camp. And because of his leadership, determination, and sportsmanship, Michael was named a captain during his senior year.

It's Michael's courage that has the greatest impact on people he meets. Michael accepts his limitations, but he never stops trying to achieve more. He inspires people because he is always encouraging others to do well, looking for ways to learn more, and working hard to be better at what he does.

Excepted from www.wdeptford.k12.nj.us/High_School/Athletics/ScholarAthlete.htm.

The Courage to Love

For fifteen years Gertruda worked for a wealthy Jewish family in Poland. Then came the Nazis and World War II. First the father was taken to Auschwitz, a concentration camp. Then the daughter died. Finally the mother died, leaving Gertruda, who was a single, forty-year-old Catholic woman, with a young Jewish boy to raise.

Gertruda kept Mickey in her apartment during the war. She could have been sent to a concentration camp if anyone knew she was hiding a Jewish boy. Once Mickey got sick. The only doctor Gertruda could find was a German doctor. Gertruda told the doctor Mickey was her brother. After several visits Mickey was better, and Gertruda asked the doctor what she owed him. He said that she owed him nothing because he was grateful for the opportunity to do something courageous. The doctor knew all along that Mickey was Jewish!

When the war was over, Gertruda took Mickey to his relatives in Israel. They wanted to adopt Mickey and send Gertruda away, but Mickey chose to turn his back on what his relatives offered and stayed with Gertruda.

Excerpted from www.pbs.org/wgbh/pages/frontline/shtetl/righteous/gertruda.html

DECISIVENESS

Starring the JELLYFISH

Plot Point: We need to be steadfast in our *decision* to serve God.

Props: You'll need a piece of art paper for each box (art paper is available in craft stores), a shoe box or paper box for each child, a Bible, a picture of a jellyfish, washable art paint, paint smocks, a spatula, a bowl, wet wipes, Jell-O gelatin, and access to a refrigerator.

Setting the Stage: Prepare a one-square-inch Jell-O Jiggler for each child. To make twenty-four squares, start with two 8-serving packages or four 4-serving packages of Jell-O gelatin. Add 2 1/2 cups of boiling water, and stir three minutes or until gelatin is completely dissolved. Pour into a 13x9-inch pan, and refrigerate at least three hours or until firm. Dip the bottom of the pan in warm water for about fifteen seconds to loosen. Cut into squares, and lift from pan. Keep the Jigglers cold until you're ready to use them.

Line shoe boxes with art paper, and have the jellyfish picture handy.

Action!

Show children the picture of the jellyfish.
ASK:

- **What do you think it would be like to be a jellyfish? Let's do an experiment to find out.**

Have children put on paint smocks, then give each child an art paper-lined shoe box. Place a quarter-size dollop of paint and a one-square-inch Jell-O Jiggler in each box. Show children how to move the box so that the Jell-O rolls around in the paint.

SAY: Make your Jell-O Jiggler go straight from one corner of your box to the other. Bring it back to the middle of the box and make it stop. Give additional directions to encourage children to try to control the Jell-O Jigglers. Let the children manipulate the Jell-O Jigglers for a few minutes, then lift the Jell-O from the boxes and put it in a bowl.

ASK:
- How easy was it to get your Jell-O Jiggler to go where you wanted it to go?
- How hard would it be for us to get where we wanted to go if we were like the Jell-O Jiggler?

SAY: In some ways, our Jell-O Jigglers are like jellyfish. In the ocean, jellyfish "swim" by using a kind of jet propulsion. A jellyfish can push water out of its body, and, as water is pushed in one direction, the jellyfish moves in the opposite direction. But the jellyfish is also pushed any which way by wind, waves, and currents.

ASK:
- Why do you think the jellyfish is called "jelly-fish"?

SAY: Jellyfish aren't really fish, and they certainly are not jelly. Although they don't resemble any other animals on earth, they are related to sea anemones and coral.

More than two hundred types of jellyfish are found in the world's oceans and seas. Some are as small as a thimble. Some have tentacles that may stretch more than one hundred feet.

Jellyfish are ninety-five percent water. They have no heart, blood, brain, or gills, but they can smell and taste. Jellyfish eat small, drifting animals called zooplankton that they trap with their tentacles.

Without any brains, jellyfish can't really make *decisions* about where they want to go or what they want to do.

God did give us brains, though, and he wants us to use our brains to make choices and to make *decisions*. God wants us to *decide* to follow him and to be steadfast in that *decision*.

Read Ephesians 4:14 to the children.

 Zoom In

ASK:
- How is *not* making *decisions* for ourselves like the way the jellyfish moves?
- Think about a time you didn't know what to do—when you couldn't make a *decision*. How did you feel?
- How can God give us direction or help us make *decisions*?

 Finale

SAY: As you take your "Jell-O-fish" painting out of your box, share with a friend one way that you will stick to your *decision* to serve God.

Starring the MINIATURE GREYHOUND

Plot Point: When we *decide* to follow God, we need to stay focused on God's will.

Props: You'll need a Bible and a picture of a miniature greyhound.

Setting the Stage: No preparation is required.

  Action!

SAY: **God gave miniature greyhounds a special ability. They can become so focused on something that they practically don't see anything else around them. They're not easily distracted, and they don't want to give up until they've gotten what they set out for. A native American tribe in the Northwest valued this ability to make a *decision* and stay focused on that *decision*. To help their children develop it, they played a game called Hagoo.**

> ### Scripture Spotlight
>
> "But when he asks, he must believe and not doubt, because he who doubts is like a wave of the sea, blown and tossed by the wind. That man should not think he will receive anything from the Lord; he is a double-minded man, unstable in all he does" (James 1:6-8).

The object of Hagoo is to stay focused no matter what is happening around you. To show how focused you are, you have to keep a straight face—no smiling or laughing—as you walk down a corridor of your friends. They will help you practice staying focused by trying to get you to smile or laugh.

Have children form two lines facing each other. Have the children at the ends of the lines take turns walking down the corridor. Remind them that they should try to keep a straight face. Remind those forming the corridor that they can't touch the walker but they can make silly sounds, funny faces, and hilarious laughs as they try to get the walker to smile.

After all the children have had an opportunity to walk down the corridor, take your turn! Then have the children sit in a semicircle, and show them the picture of the miniature greyhound.

SAY: **You might think this little dog is funny looking. It might make you laugh! This miniature greyhound has very long skinny legs and a long pointy nose. Its eyes bulge a little, and it has a long tail like a rat.**

Miniature greyhounds are fun-loving dogs that stand about knee-high. They have lots of energy and can run very fast. They are also good hunters. When a miniature greyhound sees a bird or rabbit, it runs to catch it. This little dog becomes so focused on what it has *decided* to do that nothing around it can get its attention. Miniature greyhounds could walk (or more likely run) down the Hagoo corridor and never even see the people on either side.

Jesus was so focused on doing what God wanted that he let nothing, not even the cross, distract him from doing God's work.

Read James 1:6-8 to the children.

Zoom In

ASK:

- How did you feel as you walked down the Hagoo corridor?
- Was it hard to stay focused?
- What helped you stay focused?
- What distracts you when you are trying to read or study at home?
- What distracts you from following God?
- What can help you stay focused on doing God's will?

Finale

SAY: When we *decide* to follow God, we try to stay focused on God's will, as Jesus did. God gives us prayer, songs, and friends to help us do this every day. Think of one thing you can do this week that will help you stay focused as you follow God.

Let's take turns asking God to help us stay focused on following him.

Pray together before closing.

 **Starring the CORMORANT**

Plot Point: God wants us to seek his wisdom when making *decisions*.

Props: You'll need copies of a target drawing for each child, a piece of poster board and squirt guns or squirt bottles filled with water for every five or six children, a Bible, a picture of a cormorant, markers, masking tape, and plastic mats.

Setting the Stage: Use markers to draw a target on the poster board, then tape the target to a chalkboard or wall. Put the plastic mat on the floor below the target, and use masking tape to mark a place on the floor where children will stand as they squirt water at the target. Have the picture of the cormorant available.

> **Scripture Spotlight**
>
> "If any of you lacks wisdom, he should ask God, who gives generously to all without finding fault, and it will be given to him" (James 1:5).

Action!

Have kids form teams of five or six.
SAY: Today we are going to do some target practice. As you aim for the target, imagine what it might be like if you could have supper only if you hit the center.

Have team members take turns stepping up to the line and trying to hit the bull's-eye with the squirt gun. When everyone has had a turn,
ASK:
   • Was it difficult to hit the bull's-eye? Why or why not?
   Show children the picture of the cormorant.
SAY: This is a cormorant. The cormorant is a web-footed water bird found all over the world. It's very good at catching fish. The cormorant flies above the water, watching for fish. When it sees a fish, it aims its body, the way you aimed the squirt gun, and dives into the water. Some cormorants can dive almost thirty feet under water. Once it's under water, a cormorant can swim very fast with its web-feet and short legs. And the cormorant can stay under water up to a minute. If the cormorant aims well, it gets the fish it will eat for supper.

God wants us to be like the cormorant when we have a *decision* to make. As we face the ocean of choices in our lives, we need to aim for the one thing that God would have us do. If we aim carefully, he will help us succeed.

Read James 1:5 to the children.

> **Director's Notes**
>
> Experiment a little before marking the starting line on the floor, then position the masking tape line depending on the age of your group. Young children will probably need to stand just a few feet from the target. Move the line back for older children.

 **Zoom In**

ASK:

- What would happen if the cormorant didn't aim straight for the fish it wants?
- How are you like the cormorant when you really want to accomplish something?
- Think of some serious choices or *decisions* you have to make. How can you know what God wants you to do?
- When have you made a *decision* based on what God wanted you to do? Explain.

 Finale

Pass out the copies of a target drawing.

SAY: Think of some of the choices you have to make. Then think of words or a picture to represent those choices, and write or draw them around the target. In the center of the target, write who you will rely on to give you the wisdom to make those choices.

Starring the SQUIRREL

Plot Point: *Deciding* to "store" the wisdom of the Bible now will prepare us to make the *decisions* God wants us to make.

Props: You'll need a shopping bag for each child, a Bible, index cards, and markers.

Setting the Stage: Copy passages from an easy-to-understand version of the Bible, such as the New Century Version, onto index cards. Provide two or three cards per child (passages can be copied several times—all the cards don't have to be different). Your choices might include Psalm 41:1; Matthew 5:15-16; Matthew 7:20; Matthew 16:26; Romans 5:3-5; 2 Corinthians 1:3-4; 1 Timothy 6:10; and 1 John 4:8. Set the cards out on a table.

Scripture Spotlight

"Jesus answered, 'It is written: Man does not live on bread alone, but on every word that comes from the mouth of God' " (Matthew 4:4).

 Action!

ASK:
- How many of you have watched squirrels darting back and forth outside, looking for nuts and seeds?

SAY: Squirrels are very resourceful. If you've tried to keep squirrels out of a bird feeder, you know how resourceful they are! They're resourceful about finding food, and they're resourceful about finding places to hide the food until they need it. They plan for the future months in advance. We are going to try the same thing.

Like squirrels, we need to store up food for the future too. But the Bible says that the "food" we need to store is the wisdom of God found in the Bible. This wisdom is a treasure that will help us make good *decisions* throughout our lives. Wisdom from the Bible can help us when we feel sad or alone or unsure.

Have the children form groups of three or four. Give each child a shopping bag, and tell children they can "shop" for Bible verses at the table. Explain that they should look for one or two cards that they think might be especially valuable to them. When children have made their choices, have them discuss in their groups why they made the choices they did.

Bring the children together again, and read aloud Matthew 4:4.

 Zoom In

ASK:
- What would happen if squirrels didn't work so hard to gather food?
- How is gathering wisdom from the Bible like what the squirrel does? How is it different?

• What are some things you've learned from the Bible that will be useful to you this week?

 Finale

SAY: Take the Bible verses you chose home with you. Put them where you'll see them often during the coming week. Watch for situations in which you can use their wisdom.

FRIENDSHIP

Starring the CHIMPANZEE

Plot Point: We should strive to love others as Jesus loves us.

Props: You'll need a Bible and a picture of a chimpanzee.

Setting the Stage: Clear a space so children can sit on the floor. Have the picture of the chimpanzee nearby.

Scripture Spotlight

"A friend loves at all times" (Proverbs 17:17a).

 Action!

Have children find partners. Then have them sit on the floor, forming two concentric circles. One partner in each pair will sit on the inside circle and face out, and the other partner will sit on the outside circle and face in. Hold up the picture of the chimpanzee.

SAY: This is a chimpanzee, or chimp, as some people like to say, and it's one of the most intelligent animals. God made the chimpanzee very social as well as intelligent. Chimpanzees live and travel in groups, and they love to play with one another. Chimpanzees seldom fight among themselves, and they are not aggressive. Raise your hand if you've ever had a fight or disagreement with a friend. Talk about these questions with your partner.

ASK:
- **How did you feel when you disagreed with a friend?**
- **How did you solve the problem?**

Allow partners a few minutes to discuss.

SAY: God plans for us to have friends. God does not want us to fight with our friends. We may disagree with a friend at times, but a real friend will still love us, and we will continue to love that friend. The Bible tells us in Proverbs 17:17, "A friend loves at all times." And that means our friends will love us, even during times of disagreement. Jesus loves us at all times too. Even when we make

mistakes, he continues to love us. We should strive to love our friends uncondi-
tionally, just as Jesus loves each of us.

Chimpanzees spend many hours grooming one another. Let's see what that's like. **Stand and face your partner.** Have the children stand. **The chimpanzee friends work in pairs to pick through each other's hair. The chimps look for dirt, insects, leaves, or other trash. They take out anything that's not supposed to be there. Pretend to check your chimpanzee friend's hair. Are you finding anything that should be removed? Do you think this is fun? The chimpanzees seem to see this as a friendly, social activity. They seem to enjoy grooming each other.**

A sign of a good friendship is that you love someone despite that person's faults or "debris." A true friend can see the "bugs" or "dirt" in our lives and will continue to love us anyway. A good friend will "groom" us, just as the chimps groom each other, and help us remove debris from our lives.
ASK:
- **How does a good friend groom you?**

SAY: Jesus, our very best friend, loves us despite our faults. And he loves helping us become like him.

If you're on the inside circle, tell your partner something about yourself—a talent, a fault, or an interesting fact. If you're on the outside circle, listen to your partner, then say, "A friend loves at all times."

Give the children a minute to share, then have the children on the inside circle walk clockwise so that each child has a new partner. Have the outside partner share, and have the inside partner repeat the Bible verse. Continue around the circle.

SAY: A friend truly loves at all times. Our most precious example of a great friend is Jesus. Jesus will always be our best friend, and he loves us no matter what. We can be good friends by trying really hard to love others as Jesus loves us.

Have the children sit in their circles for the Zoom In questions.

 ## Zoom In

ASK:
- **What qualities does a good friend have?**
- **How is your *friendship* with Jesus like your *friendship* with an earthly best friend?**
- **How have you been a good friend to someone? How could you be a better friend?**

 ## Finale

SAY: Think of a friend who is sometimes hard to love. Without discussing names, tell your partner what you can do this week to show that friend your love.

Starring the FERRET

Plot Point: We bring joy to others in *friendship.*

Props: You'll need a Bible, a picture of a ferret, construction paper, transparent tape, masking tape, index cards, and markers.

Setting the Stage: Write the following words on index cards, one word per card: YOU, ARE, A, GREAT, FRIEND, I, LIKE, BEING, WITH, FRIENDS, FRIENDSHIP, IS, GOD'S, COOL, GIFT. Shuffle the cards.

Scripture Spotlight

"A word aptly spoken is like apples of gold in settings of silver" (Proverbs 25:11).

 Action!

Have the children make long pointy noses by rolling construction paper into cones and fastening the paper with transparent tape. Put a rolled up piece of masking tape on the end of each nose, so the sticky side of the tape is exposed.

Have the children form three teams. Put the cards on a table or on the floor where children can reach them. Show the picture of the ferret.

SAY: The ferret is a long, furry creature that loves to play, clown around, and cuddle. It's usually about twenty inches long and only weighs about two pounds. Ferrets are very curious, and they use their long noses to poke around and discover new and fun things.

With your teammates, use your construction paper nose to "ferret out" a five-word sentence about friends. You may have to trade some words so that every team has a sentence about friends. Be friendly with the other teams! (You may need to help young children read the words and compose sentences.)

After the teams have assembled the sentences,

ASK:

- **When have you had a joyful time with a friend?**

Have children form a circle. Mix up the cards, and put them writing-side down in the middle of the circle. Have children take turns using their "noses" to take a card. Have them use the word on the card to affirm the person on their right.

ASK:

- **How did you feel when you were complimented or encouraged?**
- **Which words do you use to encourage others at home, in your neighborhood, or at school?**

Read Proverbs 25:11 to the children.

 Zoom In

ASK:

- **What words are "golden" when you hear them?**
- **What is it about those words that brings you so much joy?**
- **Who says those words to you?**
- **Who can you say those words to?**

 Finale

Have each person write three or four friendly words and the name of a friend inside his or her construction paper nose.

SAY: The ferret can sense when something is wrong with its owner and is always willing to cheer its owner up. There is hardly a time when the ferret is not eager to play and burn some energy. It brings joy to everyone around it. We bring joy to others in *friendship*. Our golden words can poke comfort and encouragement into any situation. Plan to use the words inside your ferret nose to bring joy to your friends this week.

Starring the

CLOWN FISH & SEA ANEMONE

Plot Point: Friends help each other.

Props: You'll need two 5x5-inch pieces of paper and four 5-inch pieces of yarn for each child, a Bible, colored markers, a hole punch, and pictures of a sea anemone and a clown fish. (If you have fewer than five children, you may want to give each child additional paper squares and pieces of yarn.)

Setting the Stage: Punch two holes on each side of all the squares. Set the pictures nearby. Set out the paper squares, yarn, and markers.

🔦 Scripture Spotlight

"Two are better than one, because they have a good return for their work: If one falls down, his friend can help him up. But pity the man who falls and has no one to help him up!" (Ecclesiastes 4:9-10).

 Action!

Give each child two 5-inch squares of paper and four 5-inch pieces of yarn.

SAY: We're going to make a *friendship* quilt. First we need to decorate the squares, so think of two pictures or designs you can draw that will remind you of *friendship*. Give children about ten minutes to work. As they finish, show them how to use the yarn to tie the pieces together.

SAY: When you have tied your quilt pieces together, find someone else and share the task of tying both sets of quilt pieces together. Keep doing this until all the squares of our quilt have been tied together.

Hold up the finished quilt.

SAY: You helped each other so well! See what a beautiful quilt you made by helping one another! Today we are going to learn about two sea creatures that help each other live. How many of you have ever heard of the clown fish and sea anemone? Those are some pretty funny names for sea creatures, don't you think? Sea anemones look like big flowers, similar to coral. How many of you have ever seen coral? Hold up the picture of a sea anemone.

Clown fish are brightly colored fish that live near coral reefs. Show the picture of the clown fish. **When big fish see a clown fish, they try to eat it. But the clown fish knows that the sea anemone will help it. It leads the big fish right to the hungry sea anemone. The sea anemone grabs the fish with its long arms and rescues the clown fish from certain death. Then the sea anemone gets**

🎬 Director's Notes

Provide glue, scraps of construction paper or fabric, glitter, or any other craft supplies children may enjoy using as they make the quilt.

🎬 Director's Notes

Sea anemone is similar to coral, so a piece of coral would be a great visual aid! Some craft stores sell pieces of coral.

lunch! As the sea anemone eats the big fish, it leaves little pieces for the clown fish to eat.

The sea anemone and the clown fish depend on each other to survive. If the clown fish didn't lead big fish to the sea anemone, the sea anemone would starve. And if the sea anemone didn't eat the big fish that chase the clown fish, the clown fish would be eaten! They help each other. When God made

Director's Notes

If you are unable to find a picture of the clown fish and sea anemone in an encyclopedia or a book about ocean life, you may want to sketch the scene as you tell the story. It doesn't have to be perfect; it just has to give children an idea of how these two creatures work together. (See the illustration below.)

the clown fish and the sea anemone, he made them friends. He made them to need each other. Did you know God made each of us with a certain need too? We all need friends, and we need to be friends who help and care for others.

Now I want you to look at our *friendship* quilt. It's beautiful because it has all of your pictures and designs. You helped one another make a quilt this wonderful.

Read Ecclesiastes 4:9-10 to the children.

The Bible says, "Two are better than one" because we can get more done together and we can help each other when we fall. This means that we should help our friends when they have problems and cheer them up when they are feeling sad.

 Zoom In

ASK:

- How did you feel when you were working with your friends to make the quilt?
- What are some other ways people show *friendship* to one another?
- When has a friend helped you?

 Finale

SAY: We all know someone who may be going

through a hard time or may be sad or alone. Spend a moment in prayer asking God to help you think of a person you need to reach out to in *friendship*. After you have thought of someone, think of one way you can let that person know you want to be a friend who will help in times of trouble.

Starring the DOLPHIN

Plot Point: We should stick with our friends when they need us.

Props: You'll need a Bible, a white cloth, paper, tape, scissors, a picture of a dolphin, colored markers, and a bowl.

Scripture Spotlight

"A man of many companions may come to ruin, but there is a friend who sticks closer than a brother" (Proverbs 18:24).

Setting the Stage: Tape the picture of the dolphin near the front of the room, or if you're using a book, open it to the page with the dolphin. Cut the cloth into blindfold-sized strips, one for each child. Cut a slip of paper for each child in the class, write an easily-identifiable color on each slip, fold the slips, and put them in a bowl.

 Action!

Giving each student a blindfold,

SAY: **Let's do a little exercise, but first you'll need to listen to the instructions carefully. Choose a partner, and decide which partner will put on the blindfold first. Later, the blindfolded partner will draw a slip of paper from the bowl and show it to his or her partner. The seeing partner will help the blindfolded person find something in this room that has that color.**

Before you put on the blindfold and draw the slip of paper, think about ways the seeing partner can help the blindfolded partner find the color. Think of several ways, then choose one.

Allow several minutes for partners to discuss what they will do, and have some kids share what they discussed.

SAY: **The exercise is almost impossible without help from someone. You'll need your partner's help to touch the assigned color because your partner will become your eyes when you're blindfolded.**

Let's look at a picture of an animal that helps its friends when they need help. Hold up or point to the dolphin picture.

ASK:

• **What sea animal is this?**

SAY: **Unlike sharks, dolphins are not aggressive. Instead, they are known to be gentle and friendly with humans. But did you know that they also have very strong *friendships* with each other? They are known to help each other.**

ASK:

• **How do you think one dolphin might help another dolphin?**

SAY: **Here's an example: Because dolphins are mammals, they need air to survive. Dolphins are known to help a sick or wounded dolphin by lifting up the sick friend with their backs or flippers so that the sick friend can get to the surface**

and get the air it needs to survive. A dolphin will stay with and help a sick friend until the friend is well again.

Do the dolphins help each other this way because they were told to do so? No. They stick together as friends and help each other out whenever they can. Should we help each other the way the dolphins help each other?
ASK:

• What are some ways we can help each other?

SAY: God designed dolphins to stick together and work through hard times together. It's a natural response for a dolphin to help a sick or wounded companion. God designed humans to help each other out too.

Remember the blindfold exercise we talked about at the beginning of today's devotion? Do you think you could find and touch the color you're looking for by yourself if you're blindfolded? A partner can make the task a whole lot easier.

Have the partners try the methods they chose earlier. For example, a seeing partner might try providing verbal directions, another seeing partner might lead the blindfolded partner to the object, and another seeing partner might bring the object to the blindfolded partner.

Have partners trade roles and do the exercise again.

Read Proverbs 18:24 to the children.

Zoom In

ASK:

• How did your partner make the task possible?
• What are some ways people help each other that remind you of how dolphins help each other?
• What are some ways you can stick close to your friends and help them out?

Finale

SAY: Think of a time it would've helped if you had a good friend nearby to help you get through a tough situation. Then think of ways you can "stick closer than a brother" and help a friend in need this week. Decorate your white blindfold with the markers, and remember how your friend helped you find your color. Each time you look at your blindfold, remember how you're going to be a better friend.

INITIATIVE

 Starring the INCHWORM

Plot Point: We need to include God in our goals and plans.

Props: You'll need a Bible, different colors of construction paper, markers, scissors, a ruler, transparent tape or a stapler, and masking tape.

Setting the Stage: Cut 1x4-inch strips of colored construction paper. Place masking tape as far apart as possible on the floor to make start and finish lines.

 Action!

Give each child two construction paper strips and a marker. Have children write something they want to do or accomplish in the next year on each strip. Then, as you talk about the inchworm, connect these goal strips to make a chain.

ASK:

• **Have you ever watched an inchworm move?**

SAY: Because an inchworm doesn't have legs under its middle, it moves in an "inching" way by extending the front part of its body then bringing the rear to meet it so its middle squinches together. To move a long distance, the inchworm must perform this action again and again, thousands and thousands of times. But, for the inchworm, the trip of a mile or two begins with that first squinch.

Let's have a race. Line up at the starting line and try to get to the finish line first. In this race, you can only move half a foot at a time. That means each step will be half as long as your foot. As you step forward, put the middle of your stepping foot next to the toe of the other foot.

Demonstrate the foot positions several times, and have the children practice a few steps. Then have them line up at the starting line, and give the signal to go. If the start and finish lines are far enough apart, children will probably get tired of the race before they finish it.

ASK:

    • When you started the race, did you think you would ever get to the end?
SAY: Going the whole distance takes determination, and it starts with the first step. Deciding to take the first step in a long journey or to begin a difficult project is called *initiative.*

    When the inchworm sets a goal to go somewhere, it begins its journey by moving toward it. When we set a goal or make an important decision, our first step should be to talk to God about our goal.

    If we set goals (hold up the chain) but don't start with the most important step, those goals are worthless. God wants to be part of our goals, and he longs to be included in our decisions. Remember to ask God what his will is before you start inching along toward your goals!

    Read James 4:15b to the children.

 Zoom In

ASK:

    • Think of a time you set a goal and accomplished it. How did you feel?
    • How can you put God first when you make goals?
    • How can you know if what you want to do is what God wants you to do?
    • What steps will you take to make talking to God a regular part of planning your goals?

 Finale

SAY: As I read the goals you wrote earlier, let's all pray silently and ask God to be part of these goals.

Starring the GERBIL

Plot Point: We need to take the *initiative* to seek God through prayer.

Props: You'll need a Bible; a gerbil in a cage with a wheel (if possible); and, for each child, an 8½ x 11-inch piece of white paper and an 8½-inch-square piece of white paper.

Setting the Stage: Practice folding the square piece of paper to make the bird before class and have a finished product handy. Instructions are on page 47.

 Action!

Give each child an 8½ x 11-inch piece of paper.

SAY: I have instructions that show us how to make this piece of paper into a bird like this! Show kids the finished paper bird. **We're not going to bother with the first instruction, though. We'll just begin where we actually start folding.**

> ## Scripture Spotlight
>
> "Ask and it will be given to you; seek and you will find; knock and the door will be opened to you. For everyone who asks receives; he who seeks finds; and to him who knocks, the door will be opened" (Matthew 7:7-8).

 **Director's Notes**

Check with the parents of your students in advance to see if there are any gerbil owners in the group.

Read the instructions (p. 47) to the children as you demonstrate with an 8½ x 11-inch piece of paper. Have children do each fold as you demonstrate it. The instructions will quickly become confusing because the paper isn't square. At that point,

SAY: Well, I think we could work as hard as possible to follow these instructions and we're just not going to make any progress. Maybe it was a mistake to skip the first thing we were supposed to do.

Distribute the 8½-inch-square paper, and explain that Step 1 says to start with a square piece of paper. Read the instructions, demonstrate each step, and have children do each step with you.

When the birds are complete, congratulate children on their finished birds.

ASK:

• **Have you ever seen a gerbil running and running around in a wheel?**

If you have a gerbil with you, and if it cooperates, show the kids. If you don't have a cooperative gerbil, ask kids if they've seen a gerbil exercising on its wheel. Ask one child to describe what it looks like.

SAY: When a gerbil is running on its wheel, it's working hard but going nowhere. Do you suppose it ignored the first step too?

Read Matthew 7:7-8 to the children.

SAY: It's up to us to be sure we do things with purpose. We can do things with purpose if we ask God what we should do. Making the effort to start right by

asking God for direction is called *initiative*. God wants us to ask, seek, and knock on his door to find out how he wants us to live for him.

 **Zoom In**

ASK:

- What kinds of things do you think we can ask God?
- What do you think it means to knock on God's door?
- How can we take the *initiative* to go to God with everything?

Finale

SAY: God wants us to turn to him in times of need as well as in times of joy. Think of something you want to do this week. Then take a few minutes to talk to God silently about it.

—DIRECTIONS FOR ORIGAMI BIRD—

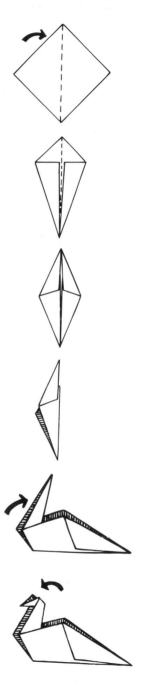

Step 1
Cut the paper so that it's square. Fold the square in half diagonally by bringing one corner of the paper to the opposite corner. Open the square back up so that you can see a line down the center.

Step 2
Place the paper so that the center fold line is straight up and down. Fold the left corner in to meet the center fold line. Crease the fold. Do the same with the right corner. Your paper will now look like a kite.

Step 3
Fold the left corner in to meet the center fold line. Crease the fold. Do the same with the right corner. Now your paper should look like a long skinny diamond.

Step 4
Turn the paper over. Fold the left corner to the right corner along the original fold line to create a long skinny triangle. The flaps are the wings of the bird.

Step 5
Place the triangle so that the longest edge is at the bottom. Pick up the corner without the flaps. Fold the corner so that it points straight up. Crease the fold. Then turn the paper over, and fold the same corner up. Crease the fold. Open and push in the triangle along the fold lines you created. This is the neck of the bird.

Step 6
Bend down the corner of the triangle that's sticking up, and crease the fold. Turn the bird over, and bend down the corner on the other side. Crease the fold. Open and push in the small triangle along the fold lines you just created. Crease the new fold. This creates the bird's head.

Starring the RACCOON

Plot Point: God wants us to take the *initiative* to reach others for him.

Props: You'll need a Bible; pencils; paper; a variety of art supplies, such as modeling clay, glue, yarn, craft sticks, and strips of leather; a picture of a raccoon; and chalkboard and chalk or newsprint and markers.

Setting the Stage: Set out the paper and pencils, but put the art supplies away in a cupboard or other storage place within the room.

Scripture Spotlight

"Therefore go and make disciples of all nations, baptizing them in the name of the Father and of the Son and of the Holy Spirit" (Matthew 28:19).

 Action!

SAY: I want each of you to design a cross. Somewhere in the room are some art supplies you can use if you want, or you can just use the paper and pencils I have here. Make your cross as nice as you can.

Give kids a few minutes to make their crosses. Don't say anything if some students do find the art supplies or if no one looks for them. Once everyone has made a cross, have kids show their crosses to the rest of the group. If someone used the art supplies,

SAY: Some of you took the *initiative,* which means you made the effort to find the art supplies I mentioned. You were able to make more interesting or realistic crosses because you took that *initiative.*

ASK:

• **Did you have fun using the art supplies?**

If no one found the art supplies, get them out and show them to the kids.

SAY: There really were some nice art supplies you could have used if you had taken the *initiative* to find them. Using these, you could have made much more interesting or realistic crosses—and you probably would have had more fun, too. Let's look at an animal that has a lot of *initiative.* Show the picture of the raccoon.

The raccoon is a curious and determined little creature and an explorer at heart. Most active in the dark, the raccoon may travel five miles in a single night, looking for new food sources and stopping along the way to investigate points of interest.

Raccoons are very intelligent and remarkably capable of getting into places people don't expect them to get into. Raccoons learn how to open latches and turn doorknobs. If a raccoon came into your house, it would probably taste everything in your cupboards.

ASK:

• **Would you taste something if you weren't sure it was edible? Why or why not?**

SAY: The raccoon is curious enough to try anything. Sometimes its curiosity gets it in trouble. Sometimes the raccoon discovers something new it likes to eat. Few garbage cans, no matter how securely closed, are able to keep raccoons out. Once the lid is off, the raccoon simply climbs inside to see what's there, often leaving a tipped-over garbage can and a big mess behind. This little animal seeks out what it wants and goes for it. There's no lack of *initiative* in the raccoon!

 Zoom In

ASK:

- How was taking the *initiative* to find the art supplies like the raccoon's *initiative*?
- What are some things God wants us to take the *initiative* to do?

SAY: God wants us to take the *initiative* to do many things. Let's look at a Bible passage that tells us about one of them.

Read aloud Matthew 28:19.

SAY: This verse tells us to look for people who need to hear about Jesus and to tell them about him.

ASK:

- When you obey this verse, how do you feel?

 Finale

Have kids brainstorm about ways they can take the *initiative* to tell others about Jesus. Make a list on a chalkboard or a sheet of newsprint. Encourage kids to commit to God to follow through on one of the ideas they've brainstormed. If you have time, let kids who didn't already do so make a cross from the art supplies. Have them take their crosses home to remind them of the *initiative* they've committed to take.

Starring the SWAN

Plot Point: God wants us to take *initiative* in helping others.

Props: You'll need a Bible and puzzles of varying difficulty, the hardest of which should take three or four children ten minutes to put together (one hundred pieces is a good limit).

Setting the Stage: Set up tables so that groups can work on their puzzles separately.

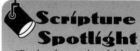

Scripture Spotlight

"Each of you should look not only to your own interests, but also to the interests of others" (Philippians 2:4).

 Action!

Have children form groups of three, and give each group a puzzle. Allow groups to work on their puzzles, but give no instructions about helping one another. Watch to see what happens when the groups with easier puzzles finish their task. Note if kids choose to help other groups or to play after completing their puzzles. Do not praise anyone for helping another group at this point. Also, don't discipline kids for playing around unless they get really out of hand.

When all puzzles are completed, praise kids for doing a good job.

SAY: It took a lot of *initiative* to complete some of those puzzles! That means completing some of the puzzles required a decision to finish the puzzle and some work to follow through on the decision. Now we're going to hear about a bird that takes *initiative* when it migrates.

The swan is a magnificent, graceful bird. It spends the warmer summer months in northern areas such as Canada and Alaska. Before winter hits, the swan joins a flock, which could include as many as five hundred swans, to migrate to a southern coastal area. Taking off slowly, these huge flocks climb to altitudes as high as six thousand feet, reaching speeds as high as one hundred miles per hour. Their trip is likely to be as long as three thousand miles each spring and fall.

How do they fly so fast and so far? By flying in a V-formation. In this formation, the swan at the point of the V takes the brunt of the wind resistance, lessening the resistance for the swans behind it. Because the lead swan works harder, the others are able to fly faster and farther. But obviously the lead swan, with its harder job, can't stay in the lead forever. As the lead swan tires, another swan takes the *initiative*, which means it decides it's ready and willing to do the work required to lead the V and make flying easier for the rest of the flock.

 **Zoom In**

ASK:

- When you finished your puzzle earlier, did any of you take the *initiative* to help another group with its puzzle? Why or why not?
- How does the swan's *initiative* when it leads the V-formation help the other swans?
- How is helping another group with its puzzle like the swans helping each other by taking the lead in the V?

Read aloud Philippians 2:4.

ASK:

- What does it really mean to look to the interests of others?

 Finale

Encourage kids to think of specific ideas in response to the following questions.

ASK:

- How can you take the *initiative* to help others around you? to help your friends? your family? people in your neighborhood? needy people in other areas?

After they've answered each part of the question above, encourage kids to think seriously about their ideas and to apply them in their lives in the coming week. If you are willing to give up one of the puzzles, give children each one piece, and have them write a few words on it to remind them of what they want to do this week to take the *initiative* in helping others.

INTEGRITY

Starring the VERVET MONKEY

Plot Point: We need to be honest so people can believe what we say.

Props: You'll need a Bible, a picture of a vervet monkey, index cards, pencils or markers, and chalkboard and chalk or newsprint and markers.

Setting the Stage: Have kids sit around tables where they can write easily.

 Action!

SAY: **I'll be giving you an index card. Think of three statements about yourself to write on your card. Two of the statements should be hard to believe but true. One statement should be false. Then write your statements on your card in any order. We'll all be trying to guess which statements are true and which are false.**

Give each child an index card and a pencil or markers, and allow a few minutes for them to think and write. (Help younger children write their statements. If your group is very young, don't require that kids write statements and read them.) When everyone is ready, have kids take turns reading aloud their three statements. As each card is read, have the rest of the group vote on which statement they think is the false one. Go around the room, and let kids have fun with this until all have read their statements.

SAY: **In this game, it was OK to be dishonest. We were just having fun together in a game. But in life, honesty is important. Let's look at an animal for which honesty is extremely important!** Show children the picture of a vervet monkey.

Vervet monkeys in their native African habitat have an elaborate communication system. They grunt to each other in greeting, and the grunts they use to greet friends are different from the grunts they use to greet monkeys they don't know as well. They also have different greetings for monkeys below and above them in the social structure.

But more important are the ways they warn other monkeys. Scientists have discovered that they make different warning calls to let other vervets know of approaching danger, and the other vervets respond differently depending on which warning sound was made. When an *eagle* warning is given, the vervets scurry down trees to hide on the ground. When vervets hear a *leopard* warning, they scramble up into the trees. At the sound of a *snake* warning, vervets stand on their hind legs and search the area around them for the intruder.

For these monkeys, honesty is extremely important. If a monkey heard a *leopard* warning when the danger was really from an eagle, the monkey might climb high in a tree and be snatched by the eagle while looking downward for the leopard. Dishonesty could mean instant death. Perhaps that's why the vervets learn which monkeys' warnings are unreliable and don't bother to respond if the one giving the alarm can't be trusted.

We need to be honest too. Being honest all the time simply because being honest is the right thing to do is called *integrity*. God wants us to honor him by being truthful with others.

 ## Zoom In

ASK:
- How did you feel when you weren't being honest in our game today?
- How could that kind of dishonesty affect you in real life?

Read aloud Proverbs 12:19.

ASK:
- How does this verse relate to the vervet monkeys?
- How does this verse relate to our lives?

 ## Finale

Have children brainstorm a list of reasons honesty is important in their lives. Write their answers on a chalkboard or newsprint. If children have trouble thinking of reasons, suggest some of the following: Dishonesty could get others in trouble, honesty helps build a good reputation, God wants us to be honest, dishonesty can hurt other people, honesty builds strong friendships, and being honest helps us honor God.

Encourage kids to think about how important honesty is in their lives and relationships. Ask God to help them be honest in every part of life.

Starring the **SEA GULL**

Plot Point: *Integrity* involves being unselfish.

Props: You'll need a Bible, napkins, and three plates or containers of treats. (The total number of treats should allow each child to have at least two.)

Setting the Stage: Hide the three containers of treats in different places in the room.

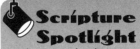

 Action!

Scripture Spotlight

"These are the things you are to do: Speak the truth to each other, and render true and sound judgment in your courts" (Zechariah 8:16).

Tell children that you've hidden treasures for them to find.

SAY: There are three separate treasures hidden around this room. Each treasure has enough treats to be shared. The object of this game is to give every person a treat as quickly as possible. When I say "go," you'll start looking around the room. If you find one of the treasures, yell, "Treasure! Treasure!" Then share the treats with anyone who responds to you. Don't eat them, though. You can all eat the treats after everyone has one.

Give the signal, and have children hunt until all the treasures have been discovered. If children seem to give up once one treasure is found, remind them that there are three. When all the treasures have been located, have each child take one. Distribute napkins if necessary. Reserve the additional treats for later. While the children are eating,

SAY: Sea gulls are interesting birds. Sometimes they seem to float through the air, sailing on the wind. At times they seem suspended in the air.

Sea gulls have ravenous appetites and will eat almost anything, from dried bread to dead fish. If several sea gulls find a single meal, such as a fish floating atop the water, they'll circle and dive to see which one of them can get to it first and selfishly fly away with it. However, if a few sea gulls see lots of food—such as when someone has put a bunch of bread out for them—they'll screech and cry out loudly. Some people think they screech to tell other gulls to join them in the feast. If only two or three gulls are nearby when you feed them, you can be sure that within minutes you'll see twenty more flying toward the food from various directions in response to the cries of the first gulls.

According to a story from history, sea gulls saved a group of Utah pioneers after thousands of crickets had appeared and were eating all of the settlers' crops. The settlers prayed, and thousands of gulls appeared and ate the crickets.

As sea gulls let other gulls know when they've found food, we can be unselfish in our relationships with others. We should be aware of what others expect of us. Part of being honest and having *integrity* is being unselfish.

 **Zoom In**

ASK:

- How did we exhibit unselfishness and *integrity* in our treasure hunt?
- How did that feel?

Read aloud Zechariah 8:16.

SAY: To "render true and sound judgment in your courts" means to be fair and honest. It means to have *integrity.* We could also say it means to be unselfish. That's part of being fair and honest.

ASK:

- How do sea gulls sometimes seem unselfish?
- What does it mean to be unselfish in your life?

 Finale

Distribute the remaining treats to the children, but don't allow them to eat them. If the treats are not wrapped, you might want to serve them on napkins.

SAY: To demonstrate the unselfishness we've talked about today, I want you to give your treat to someone else. Each of you must give your treat to one other person, and accept only one treat from someone else.

If kids do as instructed, everyone will end up with one treat. Make sure that happens.

SAY: Let's thank God for these treats and ask him to help us be fair and honest—to have *integrity.*

Pray, then allow kids to eat their treats.

Starring the SEEING EYE DOG

Plot Point: We earn the trust of others by being honest all the time.

Props: You'll need a Bible, fruit for each child, artificial fruit for every two children, napkins, and a bowl.

Setting the Stage: Set aside half of the real fruit. Put the rest of the real fruit and all of the artificial fruit in the bowl.

Scripture Spotlight

"Thus, by their fruit you will recognize them" (Matthew 7:20).

 Action!

Have children pass the fruit bowl around and each take one piece. Allow the kids who selected real fruit to eat it, while the other children hold the artificial fruit they chose. Tell the children with the real fruit not to share their fruit.

After a couple of minutes, ask the children with the artificial fruit if they got what they expected to get.

ASK:
- **How can you tell real fruit from phony fruit?**
- **What purpose does the phony fruit serve?**

Give the rest of the real fruit to the children who chose the artificial fruit, and allow them to eat it.

SAY: Have you ever seen a Seeing Eye dog? A Seeing Eye dog serves as eyes for a blind person. If the blind person trusts the dog completely, he or she can walk on busy streets, go up and down stairs, and do all sorts of things we take for granted.

The dog warns its owner of steps or curbs. The dog signals its master to stop when the traffic signal says "Don't Walk" and to go when the signal changes.

A blind man named Peter wrote an article about how much his Seeing Eye dog, Minerva, helped him. He said Minerva knew how quickly he wanted to walk and would lead him at that pace. "She would tug me across the campus at four miles an hour, ignoring the tempting squirrels who scampered across the grass but dutifully mindful of the many steps along the walk, threading her way carefully through the moving crowd of students but impatiently nudging aside the slower walkers by nosing them in the calves, hurrying across streets that were deserted but stopping short in the face of oncoming traffic." (Adapted from "The Miracle of a Blind Man and His Dog" by Peter Putnam, *The New York Times*.)

 **Zoom In**

Read aloud Matthew 7:20.

SAY: Being honest all the time and doing what you say you'll do is acting with *integrity.*

ASK:

- How could Peter know that Minerva was "telling" him the truth about when to stop and when to go?
- What would happen if Minerva decided to chase squirrels instead of help Peter?
- How can you tell which people you can trust?
- How can you show people that you will do what you say you will do?

 Finale

SAY: Think of someone whose respect and trust you would like to have. Then think of one thing you can do this week that will help that person believe in you. Find a partner and tell him or her what you plan to do this week.

Starring the CHAMELEON

Plot Point: We need to be reliable messengers for Christ.

Props: You'll need a Bible and a picture of a chameleon.

Setting the Stage: Have children gather in a circle.

 Action!

Show kids the picture of the chameleon, and ask them what they know about chameleons. After some discussion,

Scripture Spotlight

"To the weak I became weak, to win the weak. I have become all things to all men so that by all possible means I might save some. I do all this for the sake of the gospel that I may share in its blessings" (1 Corinthians 9:22-23).

SAY: The chameleon changes its color depending on its surroundings, but it is always a chameleon. It never becomes a bluebird. It never even tries to be a kangaroo. The ability to change its color makes it look like the trees where it lives or like the leaves on the ground when it's walking. We can be like chameleons and at the same time be reliable messengers of Christ so that people hear God's good news. Let's see how this might work.

Have children play Rock, Paper, Scissors making sure that all the children know the signs. Explain that the sign for rock is a fist; the sign for paper is an open hand, palm down; and the sign for scissors is extended index and middle fingers with the rest of the hand in a fist.

Have all the children count, "One, two, three," as they gently pound a fist on an open palm. On "three," tell everyone to make one of the signs.

ASK:

- **If you signed "paper," what is one thing you could change in your daily activities to help someone experience God's love?**
- **If you signed "scissors," what is one thing you would be willing to cut out of your daily life to help another person see how important Jesus is to you?**
- **If you signed "rock," what is one thing you think a Christian should never change in his or her behavior because that behavior is so important to being a Christian?**

Read 1 Corinthians 9:22-23 to the children.

ASK:
- How would you say this Scripture in your own words?

SAY: Knowing what part of your behavior should never change—and working hard to be sure it doesn't change—is having *integrity*.

Play the game again, then ask the following questions.

 **Zoom In**

ASK:
- How do you feel when people are willing to do things you like so they can get to know you?
- Have you tried to do something with someone so you could get to know that person better? What happened?
- What's the difference between being like people in order to be friends with them and being fake?
- What would you do to be like someone in order to tell him or her about God?
- What would you not change about yourself to be like someone else?

Finale

SAY: Like the chameleon, we might act different in different groups, but if we are Christians, one thing always stays the same: Wherever we are and whatever we're doing, we are Christians. If we are Christians, we can be honest because we trust in God and want God's love to show through our lives always—even when we change interests or activities so that we can be friends with people who don't yet know God.

Teach the group this prayer, using the Rock, Paper, Scissors actions.

PRAY: Lord, help me see ways each day to change [paper] so others experience your love.

Show me what to cut out [scissors] of my actions because it might be keeping your message hidden.

And give me the wisdom to stand firm [rock] and have *integrity* regarding the things that show my faith in you. Amen.

LOYALTY

Starring the SWALLOW

Plot Point: *Loyalty* means standing with those we serve in their time of need.

Props: You'll need a Bible, paper cups, Cheerios breakfast cereal, napkins, a picture of a swallow (preferably two swallows), and a bowl.

Setting the Stage: Fill cups with Cheerios so that you have at least one cup for every two children, and hide them around the room. Fill a bowl with Cheerios.

 Action!

Have each child find a partner, then have partners sit together in a circle.

SAY: We're going to play a game in which your partner will be very important to you. Turn to your partner now, and tell your partner one reason you are glad he or she is your partner. Allow a minute for discussion, then hold up the picture of the swallows.

ASK:
   • **Do you know what kind of bird this is?**
   If no one knows,

ASK:
   • **What does your throat do to get food into your stomach?**

SAY: This bird is called a swallow. Swallows depend on each other. Sometimes groups of swallows build their nests close together so they can help protect their friends if an enemy is nearby. They are *loyal* to their friends. When swallows mate, they are *loyal* to each other, and they work together to raise families year after year.

   Give each pair an empty cup.

SAY: Imagine that you are swallows and this cup represents your nest. There are four baby swallows in the nest, and they're *always* hungry. You and your partner will need to take turns bringing food back to the nest. There is food hidden

around the room. It looks like this. Show children an example of the cereal. **When you find food, you can carry only one piece at a time back to the nest where your partner is listening to the babies cry for food. Your goal is to fill the nest with food as quickly as possible.**

While you are busy collecting food, I am going to pretend to be a larger bird that's trying to steal your food.

As the children look for food, go around the room and look for unguarded cups. If children don't think of it on their own, suggest that more than one bird may need to protect a threatened nest. Encourage the children to work as a team to keep you away from their nests. After several minutes, have the children sit in the circle again.

Read aloud Proverbs 3:3.

 **Zoom In**

ASK:

- **Why is it important for swallows to help each other?**
- **Did you eat any of the cereal before you got it back to the nest? If you did, what happened?**
- **If you were guarding the nest, did you wish your partner would hurry up so you could look for food? Did you wait?**
- **Who are some people we need to be *loyal* to?**
- **How can we show *loyalty* to people who depend on us?**

 Finale

SAY: We need to stick with our friends just as swallows stick together. I have one big nest full of cereal. Show children the bowl of cereal, and distribute napkins.

I'll pass the bowl around. When the bowl comes to you, tell us one way you could be *loyal* to a friend or family member this week. After you tell us your idea, take a handful of cereal to eat.

 **Director's Notes**

Give children wet wipes, and ask them to clean their hands before they eat the cereal.

After children have finished sharing and eating,

SAY: The Bible says, "Let love and faithfulness never leave you." Let's pray: Dear God, help us to be loving and faithful friends this week. May we remember the swallow and its ability to stick with its friends. Amen.

Starring the SHEEP

Plot Point: God wants us to know him so well that we follow his lead in our lives.

Props: You'll need a Bible, a picture of a shepherd leading his flock, and masking tape.

Setting the Stage: Use masking tape to mark start and finish lines. Allow as much distance as possible between the two lines. Have children stand at the starting line.

 Action!

SAY: We're going to play a game called Shepherd Says. The goal is to cross the finish line by listening to the shepherd's voice and following the shepherd's instructions exactly. You have to listen to what the shepherd says; you can't just cross the line on your own! If you don't listen to the shepherd, you'll have to go back to the start line. Understand? OK, let's give it a try.

Shepherd says, "Walk ahead four paces."

Shepherd says, "Stand on one foot, count to three, and take one step."

"Now touch your toes, then move one step forward."

Let the kids have fun with this. Use commands such as flap your wings like a chicken, turn in a circle, sit down, make your favorite animal noise, and jump on your right foot three times. Remember to give some commands without saying, "Shepherd says."

When some kids are close to the finish line, you might want to say, "Shepherd says, skip back to the starting line" just to see if they can resist the urge to step over the finish line when they are so close.

When everyone has completed the course,

SAY: That was great! You all did such a good job! Did you see how important it was to listen carefully? If you listened to the shepherd, you completed the course. God wants us to listen to him so we can complete the course he has planned for us. Jesus compared our relationship with him to the relationship between a shepherd and his sheep.

ASK:
- What does a shepherd do?

Show the picture.

SAY: The shepherd keeps the sheep from harm. The sheep know the shepherd so well that they listen to and follow the sound of his voice. They rely on that one voice to keep them safe and in the right place. When *people* follow one voice

Scripture Spotlight

"When he [the shepherd] has brought out all his own, he goes on ahead of them, and his sheep follow him because they know his voice" (John 10:4).

and do as that one voice says, it's called *loyalty*. The sheep are completely *loyal* to the shepherd, and they will not leave him.

God wants us to be *loyal* to him. He wants us to know the sound of his voice so well that we can follow him through obstacles in our lives. When something confusing or hurtful happens, we need to listen for what God is telling us to do. **ASK:**

- How do we listen for God?

SAY: We need to be *loyal* listeners all the time because God is our leader and we are the followers. God is our shepherd; we are his sheep. We are *loyal* to him.

Read aloud John 10:4.

 Zoom In

ASK:

- What are some ways you can show *loyalty* to God?
- Is it easy to be *loyal*?
- Think of a choice you have to make. How do you know what God wants you to do?
- What do other people think when they see you show *loyalty* to God?

 Finale

Have kids find partners.

SAY: Think of a situation at home or school that will require you to listen to God and show *loyalty* to him. Tell your partner how you plan to be *loyal* to God this week.

End the session with a prayer.

SAY: Let's talk to God about it right now.

PRAY: Thank you, God, for caring for us. Thank you for loving us so much and guiding us through our lives. When we find ourselves in situations that are confusing or frightening, please be our shepherd. Please help us learn how to listen to you. In Jesus' name we pray, amen.

Starring the SEA HORSE

Plot Point: Jesus wants us to be *loyal* to one another.

Props: You'll need a Bible, a paper bag and an index card for each pair of children, dot stickers in two colors, Hershey's Kisses (or another small treat that would be difficult to divide in half), paper, markers, and a dried sea horse or a picture of a sea horse.

Scripture Spotlight

"Now it is required that those who have been given a trust must prove faithful" (1 Corinthians 4:2).

Setting the Stage: Set up the game area with one chair for every set of partners. Decide for yourself which dot stickers will represent "*loyal* to each other" and which will represent "not *loyal*," but try not to let the children know that one color is right and one is wrong. Have the dried sea horse or the picture nearby to show children.

 Action!

Begin by having each child find a partner, then have partners decide which one is Partner 1 and which is Partner 2. Give each pair one paper bag, and ask each pair to stand by a chair.

SAY: We are going to play a quick game. I am going to give you a few choices and, as I do, I'd like you to think about what you would do if this were not a game. What would you do in real life? Give each pair an index card.

All number ones, raise your hands. You get the first choice of where you want to sit. You can sit in the chair, or you can see if your partner wants the chair. When the partner decides, put the appropriate color sticker on each pair's index card.

All number twos, raise your hands. You get to decide your team's name. You can name it yourself, or you can see if your partner wants to name it. When the partner decides, put the appropriate color sticker on each pair's index card.

Number ones, one person in each pair will have to help me clean up the room before leaving today. You get to decide whether you'll stay and help clean or whether you'll ask your partner to do it. When the partner decides, put the appropriate color sticker on each pair's index card.

Number twos, you get to decide what to do with the piece of candy I'll give you. You can keep it, or you can give it to your partner. When the partner decides, put the appropriate color sticker on each pair's index card.

Give a piece of candy to the children who don't have one.

SAY: Our game was actually a little quiz about *loyalty*.

ASK:

• **What does *loyalty* mean?**

SAY: *Loyalty* means being faithful to someone who depends on you and who

you've made a promise to. Look at your card. In this game, each pair received a [color of dot sticker] **sticker for being** *loyal* **and** [color of dot sticker] **for not being** *loyal.* **How** *loyal* **were you? How** *loyal* **was your partner?**

The sea horse gives us one example of *loyalty.* Show the picture or the dried sea horse. **The mother sea horse lays her eggs in a pouch on the father's belly. The father sea horse carries the eggs in his pouch for weeks—sometimes up to six weeks—and takes very good care of them. The father sea horse is very** *loyal* **to his babies.**

Think about the game we played earlier. Were you as *loyal* **to your partner as you think a partner should be?**

Read 1 Corinthians 4:2 to the children.

SAY: God puts people in our lives and trusts us to be faithful and *loyal* **to them. ASK:**

- **Who in your life should you be** *loyal* **to?**
- **Who are some people in your life who are** *loyal* **to you?**

SAY: God is also *loyal* **to you. God has promised that he will always be with you and that he will never leave you or turn his back on you. Now that is** *loyalty!*

Read aloud 1 Corinthians 4:2 again.

 Zoom In

ASK:

- **When have you been** *loyal* **to a friend? Explain.**
- **When has a friend been** *loyal* **to you? Explain.**
- **Are there people you shouldn't be** *loyal* **to? Explain.**
- **How does it feel to know that God is** *loyal* **to you?**

 Finale

Distribute paper and markers.

SAY: Think of someone who has been *loyal* **to you. Think about how that person behaves and shows** *loyalty.* **Now think of someone you need to be** *loyal* **to. Write a note to that person, saying that you plan to be a** *loyal* **friend. Name one way you plan to show your** *loyalty.*

Starring the **LION**

Plot Point: We need to stand by those who depend on us.

Props: You'll need a Bible; newsprint; markers; and four or five miscellaneous items such as a key, a dog leash or collar, a broom, a ruler, a telephone, a tool-box, or a heart-shaped box. You'll also need a picture of lions or a stuffed toy lion.

Setting the Stage: Put all the miscellaneous items on a table so that the class can see them easily.

 Action!

Have the children form four to six groups. Have them find spaces in the room to sit in their groups and choose one team member to be the writer. Give each group a sheet of newsprint and markers.

ASK:
- **What does the word *loyal* mean?**

SAY: *Loyal* means being constant and faithful to people who trust in you.

ASK:
- **If someone is constant and faithful, would you depend on that person? Why or why not?**

SAY: As a group, think of people who depend on you. Your writer can write their names on a sheet of newsprint. (If younger children are doing this devotion, have them take turns drawing pictures of people who depend on them.) Allow several minutes for children to develop their lists, then invite volunteers to share their lists.

SAY: Look at this collection of things on the table. Hold up each item, and name it. **I am going to pass these items around. As each item comes to your group, talk about how it might represent some way that the people on your list depend on you. For example, a broom might represent how your parents depend on you to be helpful around the house.**

Give an item to each group, and tell children to pass the item to another

---

Scripture Spotlight

"If you have any encouragement from being united with Christ, if any comfort from his love…then make my joy complete by being like-minded, having the same love, being one in spirit and purpose. Do nothing out of selfish ambition or vain conceit, but in humility consider others better than yourselves" (Philippians 2:1-3).

Director's Notes

Here are some examples of how the students could respond: "The key is a reminder that my friend relies on me to keep her secrets locked up" or "The telephone is a reminder that God relies on me to talk about him." Remember that there are no right or wrong answers. Younger children may not be ready to think in symbols; expect very basic connections from them.

group when they are finished.

Give groups five or ten minutes to work on their lists. Then ask for volunteers to share. Congratulate the children on their examples, and have them sit in a semicircle around you.

Show the lion picture or toy.

SAY: Lionesses are the mother lions in large lion families, called prides, and they're very *loyal* to their prides. The lionesses see the needs of their prides as more important than their own needs. Even though the lionesses have cubs to take care of, they still hunt to provide food for their prides. Whenever the mother lion goes hunting, she has to hide her cubs in a new place so they'll be safe while she's gone. Lionesses know that their prides depend on them, so they are constant and trustworthy.

We, too, are part of a larger family—the church. Listen to what the Bible says to people who are part of God's church.

Read Philippians 2:1-3 to the children.

 Zoom In

ASK:

- What do you think it means to be "one in spirit and purpose"?
- How can we show those who depend on us that we will stand by them?
- What happens in your family if one person is selfish and doesn't think about other family members?
- How can we show our *loyalty* to God?

 Finale

SAY: Think of people who depend on you. How can you be more *loyal* to them? Quietly share your thoughts with God and ask for his help.

ORDERLINESS

 Starring the **BEAVER**

Plot Point: We need to be *orderly* and organized to use the resources God gives us according to his plan.

Props: You'll need a Bible; paper plates; stick pretzels; curved pretzels; cream cheese; plastic knives; napkins; and pictures of a beaver, a beaver dam, and a beaver lodge.

Setting the Stage: Have the props close by, and have children gather around a table or other work area.

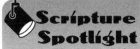
Scripture Spotlight
"Everything should be done in a fitting and orderly way" (1 Corinthians 14:40).

 Action!

Begin by showing the picture of the beaver and telling children what it is.
ASK:
   • **What do you know about beavers?**
SAY: Beavers are known for using their strong front teeth to cut down trees. After a beaver cuts a tree down, it will cut the tree into sections and drag the sections to the water. These sections are used for food and to build dams and lodges. Show the picture of a dam.

   Beavers build dams to stop the water flow of streams and make ponds; then they use the ponds to store food and to provide protection. Beavers build dams in a very methodical, *orderly* fashion. First, they use mud and stones to form the bottom of the dam. Then they add twigs, branches, and logs. Logs anchor the dam, and between the layers of logs and twigs are layers of mud to keep things in place. The beavers plaster the top of the dam with mud to make it watertight. Show the picture of a lodge.
SAY: Groups or colonies of beavers live together in lodges, which the beavers build behind their dams. The lodges are also built in a very *orderly* way.

   A beaver uses sticks, branches, and mud for the lodge, just as it did for the dam. Entrances are underwater so predators can't get to them, and tunnels lead from the entrances to the living rooms. These rooms have floors of branches and are just above the water. They are built to allow air in. Usually there is a room

for eating and a room for sleeping. In these rooms, the beavers can stay warm, dry, and safe from predators. Beavers never let their dams or lodges fall into disrepair. They are continually fixing and repairing them.

God gave the beaver the instinct to work in an *orderly* manner. God wants us to live and work in an *orderly* fashion too. Being organized and *orderly* enables us to keep our focus on him. One way to keep *order* in our own lives is to be good managers of our time.

Think about what you have to do on a normal school day. While you are at school, you work on assignments, finish projects, and participate in activities. Then you have things to do at home, such as chores and homework. You also want time to have fun.

Let's think about *order* in our own lives as we work on our version of a beaver lodge. Give each child a plate, a few curved pretzels, and a handful of stick pretzels. **See if you can stack your pretzels to look like a beaver's lodge.** Show the picture of the beaver lodge again. As the children begin to notice that the pretzels will not stack on top of one another without rolling away,
ASK:

- Who remembers what the beaver needs to build its lodge other than sticks and branches?

SAY: A beaver has a very *orderly* way of building its home. It uses mud to stick all the branches and logs together. We also need something to keep our sticks together.

Give each child a dollop of cream cheese and a plastic knife. Encourage children to use cream cheese to "glue" some of the curved pretzels to the paper plate, then glue the straight pretzels on top to resemble a beaver lodge.

As children build,

SAY: When our lives are disorganized and not in *order*, we lose focus on the important things in life—Jesus, for
example. **Organizing our time will help us keep our lives in *order*.**

Read aloud 1 Corinthians 14:40.

 **Director's Notes**

Cream cheese used as a glue for the dam will not harden, though it will hold its shape temporarily. If you do not plan to snack on the art project later and would prefer that the dam keep its shape longer, use a frosting instead.

 Zoom In
ASK:

- Are there times your life is not *orderly*? Describe those times.
- How do you feel during those times?
- How does the beaver keep his family safe and dry and well-fed?
- What can you do to change the part of your life that's not *orderly*?

Finale
SAY: Think of something you can do this week to make better use of your time so that your life is more *orderly*. Silently ask God to help you.

Starring the CHIPMUNK

Plot Point: We need to do the right thing at the right time.

Props: You'll need a Bible, slips of paper, markers, tape, treats for all the children, napkins, a box, and a picture of a chipmunk.

Setting the Stage: Put the treats in a box, and hide the box. Develop a series of clues so that one clue leads to another and the last clue leads to the box of treats. For example, write, "I have legs, but I'll never run away. When you draw or write, I'm sturdy and able. Look under my top to see what I say," to send kids to a table. The clue taped under the table might say, "I'm full of colors that are easy to hold. They break if they're stepped on, and they melt in the sun. Look inside me, then do as you're told," to lead kids to a box of crayons. Develop at least four clues or more if you choose.

> **Scripture Spotlight**
>
> "A sluggard does not plow in season; so at harvest time he looks but finds nothing" (Proverbs 20:4).

 Action!

Have children sit in a semicircle, and show them the picture of the chipmunk.

SAY: Chipmunks are very smart and *orderly* animals. They work hard in the summer, gathering nuts and seeds in their cheeks and storing the food in separate rooms in their tunnels. In the winter, chipmunks rest in the tunnels where it's warm. They can do this because they do the right thing at the right time. Chipmunks don't wait until winter arrives before they begin to gather food; they do things in the *order* that God designed for them.

God's Word gives us instructions about how to live an *orderly* life too. We just need to learn how to follow his instructions.

Let's practice following instructions now. A treasure is hidden in this room, but you'll need to do the right thing at the right time to find it. Listen to the first clue. Read the first clue. If you have more than six children in your group, have the children form teams to decide where to go for the clue. Have the group or groups come together to hear the next clue as it's found.

Have children sit in the semicircle again as you read aloud Proverbs 20:4.

 Zoom In

ASK:

- **Why does the chipmunk have to do the right thing at the right time?**
- **Why did you have to follow the clues in *order*?**
- **What other things do you have to do at the right time or in the right**

order? What would have happened if you had done the treasure hunt out of *order?*

• What are some things God wants you to do at the right time?

 Finale

SAY: Think of two things you should be doing in a fitting and *orderly* way. Ask God to help you with those two things.

Starring the STORK

Plot Point: God's Word, the Bible, outlines an *orderly* plan for our lives.

Props: You'll need a Bible, one copy of a local map for every four children, highlighters, and chalkboard and chalk or newsprint and markers.

Setting the Stage: In advance, locate four places on the map that will be easy for the kids to find, and write the locations on the chalkboard or newsprint. Have a picture of a stork available for use later in the devotional.

Scripture Spotlight

"Even the stork in the sky knows her appointed seasons, and the dove, the swift and the thrush observe the time of their migration. But my people do not know the requirements of the Lord" (Jeremiah 8:7).

 Action!

Have children form groups of four. Give each group a map and a highlighter.

SAY: Work in your group to locate the four places I've listed, then decide as a group what is the best route to follow to visit all four places. Take turns highlighting the roads you will use, and number each place to show in what *order* you'll visit the four places.

 **Director's Notes**

If the map is too complex for your group, have the kids map out a plan to visit four learning centers in your classroom by the symbols or words you use to describe them each week.

Give children time to work on the maps, then ask volunteers to share their routes.

ASK:

- **Have you ever seen a group of birds migrating south for the winter? How do you think they decide what path to take?**

Show the picture of the stork.

SAY: This is a stork. The prophet Jeremiah noticed that the stork was a very wise bird because it knew exactly where it should go in the winter and when it should migrate so it would get to a warmer climate before winter.

Read Jeremiah 8:7 to the children.

SAY: The stork knows when to move from one region to the next and how to get where it needs to be. The stork has a plan.

The Bible says that we would be wise to look at the stork and plan how best to use our own lives. God's Word, the Bible, helps us do just that.

Read aloud Jeremiah 8:7 again.

 **Zoom In**

ASK:

- How was planning the routes to the four locations on the map like deciding which direction to go in our lives?
- Do you sometimes feel you don't know what you should do first? Explain.
- How can God help us make plans so we have direction in our lives?

 Finale

SAY: God wants to give us direction. He gave us his Word to use as a map. Get together with your group and make a plan to read God's Word every day.

Starring the SPIDER

Plot Point: Making our lives *orderly* means building on the right foundation.

Props: You'll need a Bible, a long rope, and an adult volunteer.

Setting the Stage: Lay the rope on the floor in a straight line.

 Action!

 Scripture Spotlight

"Therefore everyone who hears these words of mine and puts them into practice is like a wise man who built his house on the rock" (Matthew 7:24).

Ask children to imagine the rope is a tightrope suspended across the Grand Canyon. Have each child carefully walk the length of the rope. Then have an adult volunteer help you hold the rope taut about five feet off the floor. Ask for volunteers to walk across the tightrope again. If anyone does volunteer, keep up the bluff until it's clear to the child that it's unsafe. Children will usually back down when they can't reach the rope.

ASK:
- Why was it OK to walk the tightrope when it was on the floor?
- Why was it not safe to walk the tightrope when it was held high?

SAY: Whatever we do, we want to start from a firm foundation. Think of a spider's web and how fragile it looks, yet the web is strong enough to hold a bug that gets trapped in it.

When the spider begins to build a web, it releases a silk thread that is carried by the wind. If the end of the thread becomes securely attached—to a twig, for example—the spider secures the thread and crosses the newly formed bridge, reinforcing it with additional threads. This one thread is the foundation for the rest of the web. That's why the spider makes certain it's secure then reinforces it.

When the foundation thread is set, the spider descends from the middle of it to secure a thread on the ground or on a twig. The spider climbs back to the foundation thread, carrying another thread partway across before securing it. This is the first spoke in the web. The spider repeats the process to make all the spokes in the web.

Jesus wants our faith in him to be the foundation for our lives. Then, as we follow his words, we will live our lives in a strong and *orderly* way—the way the spider builds its web.

Read Matthew 7:24 to the children.

 **Zoom In**

ASK:

- How does our faith give us a foundation we can depend on?
- How is the spider's building a web like and unlike our building on a foundation of faith?
- How can your faith make your life more *orderly*?

 Finale

Have children form groups of three or four.

SAY: In your group, discuss ways you can make sure that your faith in Jesus is the foundation for your life.

PERSEVERANCE

Starring the GREYHOUND

Plot Point: Being a Christian is like running a race that we have to train hard for.

Props: You'll need a Bible, a stuffed rabbit, a picture of a greyhound dog, and music that can be stopped and started.

Setting the Stage: Have music ready to play.

> ## Scripture Spotlight
> "Let us run with perseverance the race marked out for us" (Hebrews 12:1b).

 **Action!**

Begin by having the children sit in a circle.

SAY: Whoever guesses the animal I am thinking about gets to be first in our game. Give the clues listed below until someone guesses greyhound.

> It's a type of dog that's very fast.
> It can run long distances hunting for rabbits.
> It does not like to give up. It *perseveres.*
> This dog has a color in its name.
> Half of the name rhymes with pound.
> It looks like this. (Show the picture.)
> It has two parts to its name. The first part is "grey" and the second part is "hound."

Have the person who guessed correctly stand outside the circle. Bring out the rabbit.

SAY: Anyone sitting in the circle will now help this rabbit run around the circle. When the rabbit comes to you, pass it quickly to a person on either side of you.

A greyhound won't give up the race until it catches a rabbit. If you're the greyhound, you'll run around the outside of the circle and try to tag the person

 Director's Notes

Make sure the children do not throw the rabbit around, or the greyhound will not be able to catch it. If the greyhound cannot catch the rabbit, suggest that the rabbit is getting tired and must slow down a little.

with the rabbit. The people passing the rabbit may change directions any time they want to.

Let the children play until the rabbit is caught. Let other children try being the greyhound.

 Zoom In

ASK:
- If you were a greyhound, did you feel like giving up? Why didn't you?
- Why is it important for a greyhound to *persevere*, or keep trying?
- What are some things we need to do in our Christian race?
- Why is it important to *persevere*?

 Finale

Read Hebrews 12:1b to the children.

SAY: The Bible tells us to run with *perseverance* the race marked out for us. If you were a greyhound, your race would be to catch a rabbit. Right now your race is to follow Jesus' teachings. I am going to play music while you pass the rabbit around the circle again. When the music stops, the person holding the rabbit will tell us one way he or she plans to try harder to follow Jesus. For example, if you have a younger sister, you might say, "I could be nicer to my sister. Every time I get mad at her, I could remind myself that she is younger and I should set a good example."

After everyone has had a turn sharing,

SAY: Take a minute to think about how you could show *perseverance* this week in the race marked out for you.

After a moment,

PRAY: Dear God, please be with us next week as we *persevere*. We know you are always with us as we keep on trying, and we are thankful for that. We ask this in Jesus' name, amen.

Starring the ARMADILLO

Plot Point: We need to ask God for the strength to follow him consistently.

Props: You'll need a Bible, a picture of an armadillo, and one tube sock. You'll also need a piece of paper and two rolled and taped newspaper bats for each person.

Setting the Stage: Write the text of Philippians 1:6 on each piece of paper, then crumple the papers and stuff them in the sock. Be sure you can stuff the toe of the sock into the sock opening to make a secure "ball." If your group has fewer than eight people, crumple blank sheets of paper in a different color to fill out the ball.

> **Scripture Spotlight**
> "Being confident of this, that he who began a good work in you will carry it on to completion until the day of Christ Jesus" (Philippians 1:6).

 Action!

Give each person two rolled and taped newspaper bats, and have the group form a circle.

SAY: We're going to play a game, and the object is to keep the ball moving across the circle using the newspaper bats. If the ball comes to you, try to catch it with your bat. Then quickly toss it across the circle again, still using your bat. I think this game will require some *perseverance,* but keep trying until you can keep the sock from falling on the floor for two minutes. If it looks like your neighbor may have trouble catching the ball, you can help, but be careful and don't hit someone with your newspaper bat.

Facilitate the game, offering encouragement as needed. If the group reaches the two-minute goal easily, have everyone put down one of his or her rolled newspaper bats.

After about ten minutes, or when kids seem to be getting tired of the game, hold the rolled-up sock.

SAY: This ball reminds me of an armadillo.
ASK:
• **What do you know about armadillos?**
Show the picture.

SAY: The armadillo is an amazing creature that you might see in Mexico and Texas. The armadillo is a very timid animal that eats vegetables, small bugs, and worms. It can't see very well, so it doesn't always know that enemies are near, and it doesn't fight very well either. Unfortunately, coyotes and foxes, which have very good eyesight and are very quick, like to eat armadillos.

You might think the armadillo should just give up! But God made the armadillo with something that protects it. The armadillo has an armor plating.

When it's attacked, it can roll into a ball so the armor protects it all over. Then it just has to wait until the enemy gives up. The armadillo can *persevere* because God gave it a tool for survival.

Unroll the sock, take out one of the crumpled slips, and read one.

 Zoom In

ASK:

- **What went through your mind as you tried to keep the ball in the air in this game?**
- **What are some of the challenging tasks you face in everyday life?**
- **Where do you find encouragement to keep trying when you have to do something difficult?**
- **When do you feel like giving up? What do you do at those times?**

 Finale

Distribute the crumpled papers to the children, and have them open the papers and read the verse together.

SAY: **Think of a situation in your life in which you need God's help to keep** *persevering.*

Say to each person in the group: "God will keep working in you."

Starring the SPARROW

Plot Point: God wants us to face struggles with joy.

Props: You'll need a Bible.

Setting the Stage: Prepare an area where children can play Simon Says.

Action!

Scripture Spotlight

"Consider it pure joy, my brothers, whenever you face trials of many kinds, because you know that the testing of your faith develops perseverance" (James 1:2-3).

Play a strange game of Simon Says with your children. Begin by playing it normally, having children do the actions you describe only if you preface your direction with "Simon says." Then start changing the rules.

You might say, "Cindy says…" When kids object, explain that you like that name better and you're going to use it if you want to. Or stop and tell kids they've done an action wrong because you meant to say it a different way. When kids object, tell them to stop complaining and have fun. Then change the name before "says" again. Continue until kids protest your rule changes. The point is to get kids frustrated enough that they want to quit. After several minutes of this, have kids sit down.

SAY: We're talking today about *perseverance*—sticking with something even when the going gets tough. Let's talk about an animal that demonstrates *perseverance.*

The sparrow is a small, brown, common-looking bird with uncommon *perseverance.* Sparrows live in many countries of the world, often in the northern regions. Though some sparrows migrate south during the winter, many don't, choosing instead to stay in northern areas where the ground is covered with snow most of the winter. Since sparrows are generally seed-eating birds, snow makes feeding difficult. But some sparrows still stick it out through the coldest, snowiest winters, refusing to give in and go farther south. But do sparrows complain? No, instead they are known for their singing. A sparrow can be found singing its song in the midst of the freezing weather. Sparrows *persevere* through the toughest of seasons, and they do it with a joyful song!

Zoom In

Read James 1:2-3 to the children.

ASK:

- How did you do at *persevering* when I kept changing the rules in the game?
- How joyful were you when I caused the game to get frustrating?

- How does the sparrow manage to sing joyfully even in the midst of a cold, snowy winter?
- How can we be joyful when we're going through tough times?

 ## Finale

ASK:

- What does today's Bible verse tell us about why trials can be good for us?
- How can knowing that trials are good for us help us to be joyful when we're going through them?

To wrap up this devotion, sing a joyful song with your kids, such as "I Have the Joy," or "Joy!" Encourage kids to lean on God for their joy when life seems tough.

Starring the SALMON

Plot Point: God can help us *persevere,* even through situations that seem impossible.

Props: You'll need several skeins of yarn in enough colors so there is one color for every two children, a Bible, index cards, markers, tape, small plastic bags, fish-shaped crackers, napkins, and a picture of a salmon.

Scripture Spotlight

"Therefore we do not lose heart. Though outwardly we are wasting away, yet inwardly we are being renewed day by day" (2 Corinthians 4:16).

Setting the Stage: Before class, write the following directions on the index cards, one direction per card. Make one complete set of directions for every two children.

Directions:

- Hungry, fish-eating birds are nearby; do four jumping jacks.
- The water is polluted, and it's hard to swim; hop on one foot six times.
- The journey is long, and you're tired; jump up and down for ten seconds.
- A hungry bear is splashing in the water; spin around three times.

Wrap the different colored lengths of yarn around objects in the classroom, such as chairs, table legs, and doorknobs, so that the yarns are tangled. As you wrap the yarn, tape a set of index card directions onto each color of yarn in four places. At the end of each length of yarn, tape a plastic bag with fish-shaped crackers in it. Try to hide the end of the yarn to keep the crackers out of view at the beginning of the game.

 Action!

Have the children find partners, then have partners sit together in a semicircle.

SAY: We're going to learn about a fish that teaches us something about *perseverance.* *Perseverance* means continuing with a job or task in spite of great adversities or difficulties. Let's find out more about the salmon, and see how it is an example of *perseverance.* Show children the picture of the salmon.

Salmon are born in freshwater streams; then most salmon swim to the ocean's saltwater where they can find their food and live. The salmon then return to the rivers of their birth to lay eggs. This journey takes them through many obstacles and difficulties.

Let's see what some of those difficulties might be. Imagine that you're a salmon and it's time to swim back to the river of your birth. The time has come to lay eggs.

Give each pair of children an end of yarn, and have them follow that length of yarn. Tell them they'll meet obstacles along the way but that there's a prize at the end. Give the children time to complete the task. As the children find the crackers,

SAY: When we *persevere,* we can complete tasks and meet goals that might have seemed impossible at first. God gave the salmon the ability to *persevere.*

God gives us the ability to *persevere* too. God tells us in 2 Corinthians 4:16, "Therefore we do not lose heart. Though outwardly we are wasting away, yet inwardly we are being renewed day by day."

God wants us to keep on trying to do his work, to never give up.

Have the children sit in the semicircle again.

 **Zoom In**

ASK:

- How did you feel when you continued to meet obstacles in your path as a salmon?
- What are some difficult tasks or goals in your own life?
- What kinds of obstacles can prevent you from completing a task or meeting a goal?
- What can you do to encourage yourself to *persevere* when the going gets rough?

 Finale

Give each child a handful of fish-shaped crackers.

SAY: Think of a time you felt like giving up. How did God help you *persevere?* Share your story with your partner as you snack on the "salmon" crackers.

RESPONSIBILITY

Starring the GRIZZLY BEAR

Plot Point: We need to be *responsible* for helping others grow spiritually.

Props: You'll need a Bible; a picture of a grizzly bear; and chairs, tables, portable walls, large boxes, or whatever else is available for making a maze.

Setting the Stage: In a room near your meeting room, set up a maze for kids to walk through. Be sure to have some dead ends from which kids will have to retreat to complete the maze.

Scripture Spotlight

"From him the whole body, joined and held together by every supporting ligament, grows and builds itself up in love, as each part does its work" (Ephesians 4:16).

 Action!

Show the grizzly bear picture to the group.

SAY: A mother grizzly bear takes great care in protecting and training her cubs. She knows that without her diligent protection and training, her cubs could be killed by wolves or could starve to death in the winter. Grizzly cubs' curiosity often lands them in trouble, and they may be spanked with a swat from their mother or allowed to experience an unhappy consequence of their wrongdoing, such as getting sprayed by a skunk!

It's a mother bear's *responsibility* to prepare her cubs for the dangers they may face. It's also her *responsibility* to come to their aid when they're in danger. A mother bear will fight to the death to save her cubs from a pack of hungry wolves. Hunters know to be wary of getting close to any bear cubs they see in the wild because the protective mother bear is likely nearby.

As mother bears care for their young and want them to grow strong, so also God cares for you and your friends and wants all of you to grow strong in your faith. God wants us to help others grow in their faith as he helps us grow strong in our faith, just as the mother bear helps her cubs grow to be strong and wise.

Tell children that you're going to have them go through a maze one at a time. Tell children that the object of this game is to help the next person in line get through the maze quickly. After a child goes through the maze, have that child tell the next child in line any hints for getting through the maze. Encourage kids to listen to those who have already been through the maze.

When all the kids have been through the maze,

SAY: You helped each other learn how to get through the maze faster and faster. What you did here is kind of like what God wants us to do in real life!

Read Ephesians 4:16 to the children.

Zoom In

ASK:

- **How did you feel helping others go through the maze faster?**
- **How is helping others go through the maze similar to what the mother bear does in helping her cubs grow up safely?**
- **How is helping others like what God wants us to do in building others up in love?**
- **What can we do to help others grow in their faith?**

Finale

Have children form groups of three or four. Have them share with one another what others could do for them that might help them grow in their faith. Ask God to help the kids remember to help each other along the way as they all seek to grow spiritually.

Starring the **CROW**

Plot Point: We each have a job to do in God's plan.

Props: You'll need a Bible, paper, pencils, and index cards.

Setting the Stage: Have props ready to distribute.

 Action!

Have children form groups of four and number off, one through four.

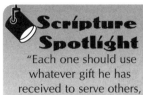
Scripture Spotlight
"Each one should use whatever gift he has received to serve others, faithfully administering God's grace in its various forms" (1 Peter 4:10).

SAY: I'm going to call each number, one at a time. When I call your number, come to me and listen to the instructions you're to follow within your group.

Call kids with each number to gather around you, one number at a time. Give them the following instructions quietly, so that kids with other numbers can't hear.

> **ONES**—Lead your group in constructing a short story about a crow that refuses to do its part in the flock.
>
> **TWOS**—Give all the ideas you can, being as helpful as you can to the number one in your group.
>
> **THREES**—Encourage all group members as they give ideas for completing your task. Try to get everyone to participate.
>
> **FOURS**—Act grumpy and refuse to do anything your group or group leader wants you to do.

Give groups paper and pencils, and allow a few minutes for the groups to complete their stories. Then have groups share their stories with everyone. Don't allow anyone to put down any other group's story.

SAY: We'll be talking more about those stories later, but now I want to tell you a little bit about what crows are really like.

Crows are extremely loyal to their flocks, and certain crows take turns doing specific jobs for the good of the flock. When a flock of crows finds a plentiful feeding site, most of the flock will descend to feed ravenously on the food. However, feeding like that—paying attention only to what they're eating—can put a flock of crows in danger from predators.

ASK:

> • What kinds of predators might attack the crows while they're eating?

SAY: To protect themselves from danger, the crows post lookouts. A few crows are always perched near the tops of trees, watching for any signs of danger. If they see danger, the lookout crows call out with a cry that warns all the other crows of danger. The lookout crows have the *responsibility* of warning the other

crows. This task is so important to the flock that if danger befalls a flock because the lookouts have not done their job, the flock will actually attack the lookouts because they didn't do what they were supposed to do.

God has a job for each one of us, and he gives us special abilities to do that job. He won't attack us if we don't do our jobs, but he does want us to take seriously the tasks he wants us to do.

Read aloud 1 Peter 4:10.

 **Zoom In**

ASK:

- How did you feel when you were in your story group and one person didn't want to cooperate?
- How are the jobs God wants us to do like the jobs of the lookout crows? How are they different?
- What could happen to the flock of crows if the lookouts didn't do their job?
- What could happen in the church community if people didn't do what God wanted them to do?

 Finale

Give each child an index card and a pencil.

SAY: Think about things you do well that might be gifts God has given you. Write down at least two on your index card. No one needs to see what you've written.

After a minute or two,

SAY: Now write on the card something God might want you to do in the church using that ability or gift he has given you.

After kids have finished,

SAY: God wants us all to use the abilities he's given us to do specific things for him. And when we do, the whole church will be better for it!

Starring the EMPEROR PENGUIN

Plot Point: We should do all we can to do what people who count on us expect us to do.

Props: You'll need a treat and a hard-boiled egg for each child, a Bible, masking tape, paper bowls or napkins, and a picture of an emperor penguin.

Setting the Stage: Use the masking tape to place small X's in various locations on the floor of the room. There should be one X for every four or five children. Have the picture of the penguin nearby to show the children later.

> ### Scripture Spotlight
> "The man who plants and the man who waters have one purpose, and each will be rewarded according to his own labor" (1 Corinthians 3:8).

 ## Action!

Have children form teams of four or five.

SAY: Today we are going to be emperor penguins with a huge *responsibility!* Emperor penguins are the largest of all penguins, and they live in Antarctica. The mother penguin has just laid an egg and has returned to the ocean to find food. It is now our job as father penguins to keep this egg safe and warm. And that's going to be a really tough job because we're in Antarctica and ice is everywhere!

Place the hard-boiled eggs in various spots around the room. Show children how to waddle to an egg.

SAY: Use your hand like a penguin's flipper and gently roll the egg onto your feet. Keep your feet close together, the way a penguin would do. Now waddle to one of the X's on the floor. You'll probably need to walk on your heels with your toes lifted off the ground to balance the egg. If the egg rolls off, stop and gently roll the egg back onto your feet.

Meet other emperor penguins from your team and huddle close together. It's your *responsibility* for the next two months to keep the egg warm and safe. You won't be able to eat at all during these two months! Have the children form small, tight circles with their eggs on their feet.

SAY: You know what? Two months is a long time. I'm getting hungry just thinking about it! Help yourself to a treat. Mention how tasty it is. Ask children if they can smell how good it is. Ask them if they've had this kind of treat before and if they like it.

Director's Notes

For the treat, try a trail mix of dried fruit pieces, raisins, nuts, small pretzels, cheese crackers, and small candy pieces. (Check with parents to be sure none of the children are allergic to nuts.)

SAY: Thinking about food must really make you hungry! But it's your *responsibility* to take care of your egg, and that means no eating for almost two long months! After two long, cold months, the eggs will hatch. Put away the treats until later.

ASK:

- What do you think the father penguin would be thinking now?
- What would happen if the father penguin went to look for food?

SAY: The eggs will hatch only if the father penguins are *responsible* and stay with them. When the eggs hatch, the father penguins feed the baby chicks milk that is produced in the father's throats. Soon the mother penguins will return to take care of the chicks, and the father penguins will go to the ocean to search for food.

Take the eggs off your feet now, and join me here on the floor. Give each child a treat in a bowl or on a napkin. As the children snack,

SAY: When the mother penguins return, all the baby chicks are herded into groups, and the parents form a circle around them to keep them warm. The adult penguins will help keep the chicks warm for six months. Then the young penguins can take care of themselves.

What a big job the penguin parents have! God gave them an awesome *responsibility*, didn't he?

God gives us *responsibilities* too.

Read aloud 1 Corinthians 3:8.

SAY: God wants us to take *responsibility* for things like taking care of our rooms, taking care of our pets, watching our brothers and sisters, and doing our work without being told. There are people in our lives who count on us—our parents, brothers, sisters, teachers, and friends, for example. These people expect us to do certain things. We can take *responsibility* to do what these people count on us to do.

After the children have finished eating, have them continue to sit with you for the following questions.

 Zoom In

ASK:

- How did it feel being *responsible* for keeping the egg on your feet?
- Who are some of the people who count on you in your everyday life?
- When is it difficult for you to be *responsible*?

 Finale

SAY: Think of a time someone gave you a big *responsibility*. How did you feel after you had accomplished the job? Share your story with someone from your team.

Starring the FOX

Plot Point: We have a *responsibility* to encourage others in their faith when they're in need.

Props: You'll need a Bible, a foam rubber ball, a laundry basket, and masking tape.

Setting the Stage: Place a line of masking tape on the floor for kids to stand behind while shooting baskets. Place the basket on the floor about six or eight feet away. (Take the ages and abilities of your kids into account. You don't want them to make a basket every time, but you don't want them to miss almost all the time either.)

Scripture Spotlight

"Do not let any unwholesome talk come out of your mouths, but only what is helpful for building others up according to their needs, that it may benefit those who listen" (Ephesians 4:29).

 Action!

Have all the kids line up to shoot baskets. However, tell kids this is not a competition of one individual or team against another. Instead, the goal is to see how many baskets they can make as a group. Tell kids to be totally silent, then give everyone one shot at the basket. Count the baskets. Have kids cheer and encourage each other, then let everyone have one more turn shooting. Don't allow any negative comments or put-downs. Again, count the baskets, and congratulate kids if they beat their first score. If not, give them one more try, still encouraging them to cheer for one another.

SAY: One way to encourage each other is by helping each other. One animal that really helps its mate is the red fox. In fact, of all the animals, the red foxes are probably the best example of animals that help each other and feel *responsible* for each other. Foxes mate for life and spend most of their time with their mates. They share the *responsibility* of raising their pups, as some other animals do. But even beyond that, foxes try to help each other when the need arises. If one mate gets in trouble, the other will often help.

For example, foxes have even been known to help each other when one is being chased by dogs in a fox hunt. Foxes typically run in circles of a mile or more when they're being chased. If one fox is being chased, its partner may hide so that the fox that's being chased can run past the hiding spot. Then the rested mate jumps out so the dogs will chase it while the first fox rests. By taking turns helping each other in this way, the foxes can keep running until the dogs tire and give up the chase. Show children the illustration on page 92.

God wants us to help and encourage each other with our actions and words. Read Ephesians 4:29 to the children.

 **Zoom In**

ASK:

- What does this verse say we're to do for each other?
- How did it feel when others were cheering for you to make a basket?
- How was the cheering like what foxes do to help each other?
- How do you encourage friends in their faith?

 Finale

Have kids form groups of about four, and have kids encourage each other in the groups. For example, they might say, "I really like the way you shoot baskets" or "Your hair looks really nice today." Tell kids to be sincere, and make sure they don't tease or put others down. Wrap up the devotion by leading this cheer: "Let's go for God!"

SELF-DISCIPLINE

Starring the GROUNDHOG

Plot Point: God wants us to keep our relationship with him in tiptop shape.

Props: You'll need a Bible.

Setting the Stage: Prepare an area where children can do the exercises described without bumping into each other.

 Action!

Scripture Spotlight

"Everyone who competes in the games goes into strict training. They do it to get a crown that will not last; but we do it to get a crown that will last forever" (1 Corinthians 9:25).

Begin by having children do some calisthenics. For example, have them stand and do ten jumping jacks. Have them sit and do ten sit-ups. Then have them stand again and do ten toe-touches.

SAY: Doing all those exercises was a lot of work!

Have children form groups of three or four.

SAY: Talk for a minute in your group about why people exercise.

After a minute, ask volunteers to report what their groups discussed.

SAY: People exercise to keep their bodies fit—in tiptop shape. Without exercise, our muscles will not be strong, and we won't be able to run as fast or walk as far as we should be able to.

There's an animal called a groundhog that has its own way of keeping fit. No, it doesn't do jumping jacks or toe-touches, but it keeps itself and its home neat and fit all the time. The groundhog probably keeps its home neater than you keep your room!

Groundhogs live in burrows under the ground. Do you think a home in the dirt underground would be very clean?

The groundhog keeps its home clean and tidy. It brings dry grass into its home to make a nest for sleeping. When the grass gets dirty, the groundhog takes the old grass out and gets clean grass. When the groundhog has to go to the bathroom, it leaves its living space and digs a hole. When it finishes, it covers the hole up, then packs the dirt down over it. The groundhog keeps itself clean, too, by keeping its fur clean of any dirt or grass that might easily stick to it. Does all that sound like a lot of work?

The groundhog is *self-disciplined* in keeping itself and its living area in tiptop shape.

God wants us to be tidy in the way we live too. But even more important is that he wants us to keep our relationship with him in tiptop shape. Paul, one of the Bible writers, talks about keeping his relationship with God in shape kind of like the way we talked earlier about keeping our bodies in shape.

Read aloud 1 Corinthians 9:25.

SAY: Paul isn't talking about training to keep his body fit. He's talking about *disciplining* himself to keep his relationship with God tuned up. We can do that by praying, reading our Bibles regularly, and doing what we know God wants us to do.

 **Zoom In**

ASK:

- How did you feel after exercising earlier?
- What do you do to make your relationship with God stronger?
- How is the groundhog's keeping its home in tiptop shape like our keeping our relationship with God in tiptop shape?

 Finale

SAY: Choose an area of your relationship with God that you think isn't quite in tiptop shape. Maybe you haven't read your Bible for weeks. Or maybe you lied to your mom about something. Ask God to help you do what you need to do to keep your relationship with him in great shape!

 Starring the **GREAT HORNED OWL**

Plot Point: We must not let temptations draw us away from God.

Props: You'll need a Bible and a bowl. You'll also need at least three foil-wrapped candy eggs or other wrapped candy for each child.

Setting the Stage: Arrange chairs in a circle at least ten feet across if the space allows it. Place the candy in a bowl.

 Action!

> **Scripture Spotlight**
>
> "Be self-controlled and alert. Your enemy the devil prowls around like a roaring lion looking for someone to devour" (1 Peter 5:8).

Have children sit in chairs in the circle. Give each child a candy egg from the bowl. Then place the bowl in the middle of the circle.

SAY: When I say "go," you may leave your seat to come and get one more candy out of the bowl. However, you must leave the candy egg I've already given you on your chair. You are not allowed to carry it with you or to hide it. When you leave your seat, you may also take any candy eggs you find on other chairs.

Repeat the instructions so that kids understand them, then give the "go" signal and see what happens. Some children may go for the candy in the bowl; others may stay back to grab candy off chairs. Still others may just sit tight with the candy they have. If no one moves, tempt the children more by telling them they can take *two* pieces if they come to the bowl. After a minute, end the game. Ask for volunteers to explain what they chose to do.

Make sure the candy is distributed equally among the children, and allow them to eat it as you continue.

SAY: The temptation we just experienced in this game is kind of like the temptation a mother great horned owl experiences as she sits on her eggs to keep them warm until they hatch.

The great horned owl lays her eggs in the winter, much earlier than most other birds, even in areas where cold and snow chill the air for months. And once the eggs are laid, the owl dares not leave her nest for long because of the danger of the precious eggs freezing. Instead, the mother owl almost gives up eating for a month—the time she has to sit on the eggs. She stays put, covering the eggs even when it snows, blanketing her in white. No doubt she gets hungry, but her *self-discipline* keeps her from leaving the nest. She resists the temptation to leave her nest because she won't risk losing her babies.

God wants us to be *self-disciplined* and able to resist temptation too.

Read aloud 1 Peter 5:8.

Zoom In

ASK:

- What does it mean to be *self-disciplined* and alert?
- How is being *self-disciplined* and alert like the mother owl?
- How does the activity with the candy relate to resisting temptation by being *self-disciplined*?
- What does it mean that the devil is looking for someone to devour?

Finale

ASK:

- What kinds of temptations are problems for kids your age?
- What can happen if you aren't *self-disciplined* and you give in to temptations?

SAY: Think about what temptation is hardest for you to resist. Silently tell God what that is, and ask him to help you be *self-disciplined* this coming week so that you can resist that temptation.

Starring the SEA TURTLE

Plot Point: We should do what needs to be done to achieve our goals.

Props: You'll need a Bible, a picture of a sea turtle, masking tape, and posters with these words or matching pictures: watching television, playing with friends, reading the comics, and playing video games.

Setting the Stage: Before class, use the masking tape to hang the posters in five different stations in the room.

Scripture Spotlight

"But one thing I do: Forgetting what is behind and straining toward what is ahead, I press on toward the goal to win the prize for which God has called me heavenward in Christ Jesus" (Philippians 3:13b-14).

 Action!

Begin by gathering the children in the middle of the room. Hold up the picture of the sea turtle.

ASK:
- **Who can tell me what this animal is?**

SAY: That's right; this is a sea turtle. A sea turtle's arms and legs are flippers that pull its big, heavy body through the water. When the turtle is in the water, it can swim with great speed because the water supports the heavy body and large shell. On land, though, it's slow and clumsy. Sea turtles prefer to be in the water.

However, sea turtles have to lay eggs on the beach. They lay their eggs high above the tide mark, in a deep hole dug in the sand, to protect them from too much water and from birds, raccoons, or other animals that might want to eat the eggs.

We're going to talk more about what life must be like for a mother sea turtle, but first I want you to think of a task or goal that you would like to achieve. You might think about getting good grades, behaving well at home, or being a good athlete. Take just a minute to think of your goal and have that in mind as we talk about the turtle. (Pause.)

The mother turtle starts her journey to the shore from deep in the ocean. Lead the children to the first station (watching television), but do not call attention to the poster yet.

SAY: Imagine the sea turtle looking at the vast ocean ahead of her. She has many miles to go. Does she think about stopping and giving up? She could have more fun staying deep in the ocean.

ASK:
- **What would happen if she didn't go ashore?**

SAY: Now think about your own goal, and let's look at a distraction. Have someone read the words on the poster or describe the picture.

ASK:
- **Will watching television help you achieve your goal?**
- **Do you want to forget your goal and stay here?**

SAY: Let's choose to press on and swim a little farther. Lead children to the next station (playing with friends).

SAY: The sea turtle has finally made it to land, but her large body makes crawling on land difficult. It seems so different here, kind of scary. Maybe she should turn around and go back.

Have a child read the poster or describe the picture.

ASK:
- **How easy or hard is it to tell your friends you can't play with them because you have something more important to do?**
- **What do you suppose your friends would think if you said you couldn't play because you wanted to do something else?**

As you lead children to the next poster (reading the comics),

SAY: Let's keep going. But this sandy beach hurts the turtle's flippers, and the high tide mark where she needs to lay her eggs is so far away.

Wow! Making a deep hole for the eggs and covering up the hole require lots of digging. It's just too much work, don't you think?

ASK:
- **Who would ever know if the hole wasn't very deep?**

Have a child read the distraction or describe the picture on the poster.

ASK:
- **How could taking a short break to read just one page of your comic book keep you from doing what you set out to do?**

SAY: Now that a deep hole has been prepared and the eggs are in it and all covered with sand, returning to the sea is necessary for the turtle's survival. But the sea is so far away. Maybe she could just rest awhile.

ASK:
- **What would happen if the turtle rested now that most of the work is done?**

Have a child read the distraction on the poster (playing video games) or describe the picture.

ASK:
- **What could be wrong with taking a quick break now that you've almost achieved your goal?**

Lead the children back toward the middle of the room where the activity began.

SAY: We finally made it!

Read aloud Philippians 3:13b-14.

 **Zoom In**

ASK:

- When do you need *self-discipline* in your life?
- How is that like the sea turtle's journey to lay her eggs ashore?
- Think of a time you showed *self-discipline*. Did it help you accomplish something? How did you feel about that?

 Finale

Have the children find partners.

SAY: Think of a goal that you want to achieve this week and at least one distraction you'll have to avoid. Share your goal and your distraction with your partner. Then pray silently, asking God to help your partner use *self-discipline* during this week.

Starring the HORNBILL

Plot Point: When we choose to follow Jesus, we commit to trying every day to be like him.

Props: You'll need a Bible, index cards, markers, napkins, a picture of a hornbill, small wrapped candies or some other treat, and paper lunch bags in two or three sizes or two or three colors. You'll need one paper bag for each child.

> **Scripture Spotlight**
>
> "Jesus replied, 'No one who puts his hand to the plow and looks back is fit for service in the kingdom of God' " (Luke 9:62).

Setting the Stage: Put one piece of candy in each paper lunch bag, and group the lunch bags according to size or color to suggest that they do not all have the same contents.

Action!

SAY: I'm going to give each person a bag with something good inside it. Before I do, decide if you will keep it for yourself or if you will share it. Stand up if you plan to share what's in your lunch bag; sit if you are going to keep it for yourself.

Distribute lunch bags and allow children to see what's in them. Ask them not to say anything about the contents.

SAY: Now do you want to stay with your original decision? You can change your mind if you want.

When kids have decided, have those who chose to share give their bags to others who made the same choice. Be sure everyone ends up with a bag. While children are eating,

SAY: We make choices every day that either help us do what God wants or keep us from achieving God's goals. Sometimes we have to give up something we want, or not do something we would like to do, so that we can do what God wants us to do. Show the picture of the hornbill.

What hornbills love to do is fly freely, but, for a period of time, they give up their freedom to give birth to and care for their young. The mother hornbill finds a hole in a tree and moves into it. With the help of her mate, she closes all but a narrow slit in the hole. She lays her eggs and waits for them to hatch. The male hornbill faithfully brings her food.

ASK:

- **What would happen if the mother hornbill changed her mind as she waited for the eggs to hatch? What if she just flew away?**

SAY: When the babies hatch, the mother hornbill pulls out her own pointed wing feathers so they won't stab her babies. This makes her even more vulnerable because she can no longer fly. She is willing to give up what she has for the benefit of her babies. Once her little ones have grown old enough to learn to fly,

the mother breaks open the hidden nest. By that time, her own feathers have grown back enough that she, too, can fly.

Read aloud Luke 9:62.

Zoom In

ASK:

- How did you feel when I asked you if you would share something you had when you didn't know what you'd be giving up?
- Did your feelings change when you opened your lunch bag and saw something you would really like to keep? If so, how?
- What does it mean to be willing to do what we should and not just what we want to do? to do what God wants us to do?
- How is this like what the mother hornbill does?

Finale

SAY: God designed the hornbills to have the *self-discipline* to care for their offspring—to do what they need to do and not just what they want to do. We can follow that example by caring for others in our daily lives.

Provide index cards and markers.

SAY: Think of one thing you know you should do, but isn't easy to do, to be more like Jesus. Write one or two words on your card to remind you, and put the card in the bag. Take the bag home, and put it in a place you'll see this week so you can peek inside the bag to remind yourself what you should be doing.

WORK

Starring the WHITE PELICAN

Plot Point: When the *work* is worth doing, we need to *work* at it resourcefully.

Props: You'll need ten toothpicks and a handful of mini-marshmallows for each child. You'll also need a Bible and a picture of a white pelican.

Setting the Stage: Set up tables where the children will work. Have the pelican picture nearby to show the children.

Scripture Spotlight

"Whatever you do, work at it with all your heart, as working for the Lord, not for men" (Colossians 3:23).

 Action!

ASK:

* What do you know about the Empire State Building? What is special about it?

As you give each child ten toothpicks and a handful of mini-marshmallows,

SAY: I have a task for you. Try to build a tall tower using the toothpicks and marshmallows. Allow the children five minutes to complete their towers.

ASK:

* Was it difficult to build your tower? Why?

Director's Notes

You may need to give the children some hints on how to build the towers. Make the base with four toothpicks and marshmallows and build up from there.

SAY: Just as you faced difficulty building your tower, pelicans face difficulty in their *work.* You know, it can be very difficult to catch fish when you are in the air and the fish are in the water! Show children the picture of the white pelican.

Has anyone seen a white pelican? One special thing about these birds is the way they *work* to catch fish to eat. Pelicans often fish in groups because they can gather more fish if they *work* together than if they *work* alone. They swim along the top of the water in a long line, chasing the fish. When they have chased the fish into shallow water, the pelicans circle around the fish and scoop them up in their big beak pouches.

The Bible says, "Whatever you do, work at it with all your heart, as working for the Lord, not for men." White pelicans *work* hard and persevere until they all have caught enough fish for the entire group to eat. God created them to *work* hard to get the job done so that all the pelicans in the group would have enough to eat.

God created you to do many things. God knows that you mess up sometimes, and he knows that you are not perfect. But perfection is not what God expects from you. The one thing he does ask is that you do your best.

ASK:

- Did any of you feel like giving up while you were *working* on your tower? Explain.
- What are some other things you've *worked* on that made you feel like giving up?

SAY: The white pelicans *work* together so that they can help and encourage one another. We can help and encourage one another just as the pelicans do. When you see a friend who is about to give up, encourage your friend to finish the *work* God has given him or her! Even when we feel like giving up, God wants us to keep on trying.

Form groups of four, and put your tower-building supplies together. *Work* together to build a tower using all the toothpicks and marshmallows. Give the children five minutes to work on their towers. When they have finished, give them the opportunity to show their towers to the other groups.

Read aloud Colossians 3:23.

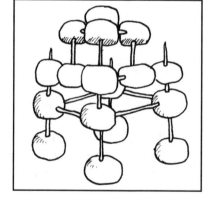

 Zoom In

ASK:

- When you *worked* as a group, were you able to build bigger, stronger, and taller towers? How did it feel to *work* on your tower as part of a group?
- How can you encourage your friends in their *work*?
- When is it hard for you to *work* "with all your heart, as working for the Lord"?

 Finale

SAY: Take a minute to think of something you have given up on or have not tried your hardest to do. Think of a way you can improve, and ask God to help you be a better worker in that area.

Starring the **ANT**

Plot Point: We should strive to *work* hard now so we'll be ready for the future God has in mind for us.

Props: You'll need a blindfold for each child, three paper cups, a Bible, two buckets of dried beans, two empty buckets, grapes, a bowl, napkins, several feet of newsprint, and lemon juice.

Setting the Stage: Place the buckets of beans at one end of the room and the empty buckets at the other end of the room. Squeeze a trail of lemon juice the length of the newsprint, and set it aside for use later in the devotion.

> ### Scripture Spotlight
> "Go to the ant, you sluggard; consider its ways and be wise! It has no commander, no overseer or ruler, yet it stores its provisions in summer and gathers its food at harvest" (Proverbs 6:6-8).

 Action!

Form two teams. Give one paper cup to Team 1 and two paper cups to Team 2. **SAY: Let's see if you can use your cup to move all the beans from your team's full bucket to your team's empty bucket.**

> ### Director's Notes
> Use a cotton swab or a dropper to make the lemon juice trail.

We'll try two methods. Team 1, stand in a straight line between the empty bucket and the bucket of beans. The person standing next to the bucket of beans will fill the cup with beans, then pass the cup to the next person, who will pass it to the next person until the cup reaches the person next to the empty bucket. That person will pour the beans into the empty bucket then start passing the cup back to the bucket of beans.

Team 2, you'll each start by your team's empty bucket. The first person will run to the other bucket of beans, fill the cup with beans, and run back to drop the beans into the empty bucket. As soon as the first person has filled the cup, the next person can run to the bucket of beans with the other cup.

> ### Director's Notes
> Show the kids in Team 2 how to run in an oval, starting on one side of the empty bucket and returning to the other side to reduce the risk of collisions.

The goal is to *work* hard to not let any beans drop on the floor. Ready? Go!
Allow kids a few minutes to complete their task.
SAY: It's obvious which team had an easier time!
ASK:

- **Which team do you think *worked* the way a colony of ants does when collecting food?**

SAY: Each ant has a specific job to do. For example, every colony has a scout

ant. It's the scout's job to find food. As the scout is searching for food, it leaves a scent behind so it can find its way back to the colony.

When the scout has found food, it sends out a signal to the worker ants to gather the food.

ASK:

• How do you think the worker ants find the food?

SAY: The workers follow the scent left by the scout. Then they all *work* together to carry the food back to the colony.

God gave us the example of ants. Not only does he want us to *work* hard, he wants us to *work* together! The team that *worked* together discovered that the *work* wasn't very hard. But the people on the team that didn't *work* together were tired when they were finished.

Let's see what it's like to *work* like an ant. Have children line up in single file. Pull out the long sheet of newsprint that you scented with a trail of lemon juice, and place a bowl of grapes at the far end of the newsprint. Give the children blindfolds, and have them crawl blindfolded, one at a time on the newsprint, following the scent to the grapes. Ask them to wait until everyone is at that end before they eat any grapes.

Read Proverbs 6:6-8 to the children.

 ## Zoom In

ASK:

• What can we learn from the way ants *work*?
• How can you *work* the way an ant does?
• What *work* do your parents need you to do?

 ## Finale

SAY: Think of a task you need to do that you've not done. As you eat your grapes, ask a friend to pray that you will *work* like an ant to finish the task.

Starring the BEE

Plot Point: We should always do our best for the Lord because the *work* we do for God always has results.

Props: You'll need a Bible; ice cream; a variety of toppings such as syrups, chopped nuts, fruit, cherries, and whipped cream; ice cream scoops; index cards; a bowl, spoon, and napkins for each student; tape; a jar of honey; and a flower.

Scripture Spotlight

"Always give yourselves fully to the work of the Lord, because you know that your labor in the Lord is not in vain"
(1 Corinthians 15:58b).

Setting the Stage: Write instructions on the index cards as follows:

Card #1: Put one large scoop of ice cream in each bowl, then pass the bowl to the next worker.

Card #2: Pour [1st] syrup [or topping] onto ice cream. Pass the bowl to the next worker.

Director's Notes

Be sure to find out if any of your students are allergic to any food, such as nuts, prior to class.

Card #3: Pour [2nd] syrup [or other topping] onto ice cream. Pass the bowl to the next worker.

Card #4: Add whipped cream. Pass the bowl to the next worker.

Card #5: Sprinkle a spoonful of chopped nuts onto the whipped cream. Pass the bowl to the next worker.

Card #6: Put a cherry on top of each sundae. Pass the bowl to the next worker.

Card #7: Put one spoon in each bowl, and set the bowl on the table.

Have enough workstations and instructions so that no more than three children work together at a workstation.

Set up workstations with supplies, and tape each instruction card in front of the corresponding station.

 Action!

Point out the workstations.

SAY: I have an assembly line set up here, but it needs some workers. Ask for volunteers for each station. When children are at their posts, point out the instructions.

SAY: Take a moment to read your instructions and discuss your assignment with your group. (You may want to read the instruction cards to younger children and make sure they know what they're supposed to do.) After a minute or two,

SAY: If you all do your *work* fully, we'll all have treats in a few minutes.

Show the group the jar of honey and a flower.

ASK:
- **Where does honey come from?**

SAY: Bees—specifically honeybees—make honey.

ASK:
- **Does anyone know how the bees make honey and why they make it?**

SAY: **They make it from the nectar of flowers.** Show children the flower. **Honey is used to feed the larvae, or baby bees.**

Take a few moments to discuss with your group what might happen if the bees didn't do their *work* of gathering nectar and making honey.

After a few minutes, ask for volunteers to share what their groups discussed.

SAY: **The bees know that they must do their best every day at gathering the nectar from flowers or the larvae will die. None of the bees' *work* is in vain; all their *work* has results.**

The bees don't stop *working* because they know that the *work* they do will help their hive survive. Just like the bees, we should always do our *work* to the best of our abilities because God will always use our *work* for his kingdom. None of the *work* we do for God goes to waste or is in vain. It always has results.

Have the groups begin running the assembly line. Once enough sundaes are made for each student to have one, ask everyone to take a sundae and to form a semicircle in front of you. Allow children to begin eating their sundaes while you read 1 Corinthians 15:58b to them.

 Zoom In

ASK:
- **How did you feel when I told you that if you did not do your *work* fully, we would not be able to eat the results of our assembly line?**
- **What would happen if a bee did not do its best *work*?**
- **When is it hard for you to do your best *work* for the Lord?**
- **How can you do a better job?**

 Finale

SAY: **Think of a situation in which you need to do your *work* fully. As you finish up your sundae, talk in your group about how you might do a better job in your *work* for the Lord. Tell your group that your *work* for God will not be wasted or in vain.**

Starring the CUCKOO BIRD

Plot Point: We will win the respect of others when we do good *work.*

Props: You'll need a Bible and music that can be stopped and started.

Setting the Stage: Arrange chairs in a circle for a game of Musical Chairs.

 Action!

Tell children that they are going to play Musical Chairs. **SAY: For this game, you need to think of your chair as a nest. Let's think about how birds build nests. Sparrows' nests are made of straw and feathers, and** they're often stuffed into the corners of roofs. Robins use twigs, roots, grass, and paper to build their nests in trees or on building ledges. Then they line the whole nest with mud. Swallows use mud to build their nests, and they reinforce the mud with straw, horsehair, or grass. They might also line their nests with feathers or soft grass.

Think about what your nest looks like. If you were a bird, you would have *worked* very hard to gather the materials and build the nest.

Now, when the music starts, stand up and move behind the nests. When the music stops, quickly find a nest to sit on.

Remove only one chair for the entire game. Start the music, then stop the music. Have all the children circle the chairs each time you start the music. Play the game a few times.

SAY: As you moved from nest to nest, you were like the cuckoo bird. Cuckoo birds don't build their own nests. They are lazy and lay their eggs in nests that other birds build. Then the nest builders sit on the cuckoo eggs, along with their own eggs, and hatch them. Sometimes the baby cuckoo birds are bigger than the nest builders' own babies, and baby cuckoos eat all the food. The nest builders' own babies can be pushed out of the nest or die of starvation.

> ## Scripture Spotlight
>
> "Make it your ambition to lead a quiet life, to mind your own business and to work with your hands...so that your daily life may win the respect of outsiders and so that you will not be dependent on anybody" (1 Thessalonians 4:11-12).

> ## Director's Notes
>
> Check your library for a video about birds of prey, then see if it shows a cuckoo bird laying an egg in another bird's nest. A short clip showing the cuckoo bird laying her eggs in another bird's nest would be a nice addition to this lesson.

ASK:

- If you were a nest builder, how do you think you'd feel about having to raise another bird's baby?
- What do you think of the cuckoo bird and the way it steals places in nests?

Read 1 Thessalonians 4:11-12 to the children.

 Zoom In

ASK:

- What are some things people do that are like what the cuckoo does when it lays eggs in other birds' nests?
- What does it mean to not be dependent on anyone?
- What are some things you *work* hard at? Do you think people respect you for doing those things?
- How do you think your hard *work* can help others understand God better?

 Finale

SAY: Think of three things you can do this week that will show others that you are a hard worker and worthy of their respect. Silently ask God for help with doing those three things to the best of your ability.

SCRIPTURE INDEX

Exciting Resources for Your Children's Ministry

Sunday School Specials Series

Lois Keffer

This best-selling series is a lifesaver for small churches that combine age groups...large churches that host family nights...and small groups with kids to entertain. Each book provides an entire quarter of active-learning experiences, interactive Bible stories, life applications, and take-home handouts. Children love them because they're fun and you'll love the easy preparation!

Sunday School Specials	ISBN 1-55945-082-7
Sunday School Specials 2	ISBN 1-55945-177-7
Sunday School Specials 3	ISBN 1-55945-606-X
Sunday School Specials 4	ISBN 0-7644-2050-X

The Children's Worker's Encyclopedia of Bible-Teaching Ideas

You get over 350 attention-grabbing, active-learning devotions...art and craft projects...creative prayers...service projects...field trips...music suggestions...quiet reflection activities...skits...and more—winning ideas from each and every book of the Bible! Simple, step-by-step directions and handy indexes make it easy to slide an idea into any meeting—on short notice—with little or no preparation!

Old Testament	ISBN 1-55945-622-1
New Testament	ISBN 1-55945-625-6

5-Minute Messages for Children

Donald Hinchey

It's easy to share meaningful messages that your children will enjoy and remember! Here are 52 short, Bible-based messages for you to use in Sunday school, children's church, or midweek meetings.

	ISBN 1-55945-030-4
5-Minute Messages and More	ISBN 0-7644-2038-0

Just-Add-Kids Games for Children's Ministry

If your classroom is stocked with the basics (chairs, paper, a light switch and masking tape) then you've got everything you need to play dozens of great new games! You get high-energy games...low-energy games...and everything in between. Some games have Bible applications, some require no supplies at all, and every game takes just moments to explain.

ISBN 0-7644-2112-3